PRACTICE MAKES PERFECT™

English Conversation

Jean Yates, PhD

McGraw Hill

New York Chicago San Francisco Lisbon London Madrid Mexico City
Milan New Delhi San Juan Seoul Singapore Sydney Toronto

5 6 7 8 9 10 11 12 13 14 15 QVS/QVS 1 9 8 7 6 5 4 3

ISBN   978-0-07-177085-9
MHID   0-07-177085-2

e-ISBN   978-0-07-177086-6
e-MHID   0-07-177086-0

Library of Congress Control Number   2012931072

McGraw-Hill, the McGraw-Hill Publishing logo, Practice Makes Perfect, and related trade dress are trademarks or registered trademarks of The McGraw-Hill Companies and/or its affiliates in the United States and other countries and may not be used without written permission. All other trademarks are the property of their respective owners. The McGraw-Hill Companies is not associated with any product or vendor mentioned in this book.

McGraw-Hill products are available at special quantity discounts to use as premiums and sales promotions or for use in corporate training programs. To contact a representative, please e-mail us at bulksales@mcgraw-hill.com.

This book is printed on acid-free paper.

Contents

Preface

Practice Makes Perfect: English Conversation is designed to give you practice with the vocabulary and structures that are most often used in common types of informal conversations.

The book consists of thirteen chapters, each one devoted to a particular conversational function. Each chapter begins with a typical conversation followed by a discussion of vocabulary and structures that are particularly important for the type of conversation being addressed. Certain expressions are repeated in other chapters so that you will become more familiar with them as they occur in different contexts. Following the discussion section are several sets of exercises to help you feel confident that you understand the material. The exercises also give you practice in using new vocabulary and structures so that you will be able to include them in your personal conversations.

Use this book, practice your English in conversations with your English-speaking friends, and continue to enjoy this language.

English Conversation

Introducing yourself and others

Conversation: Meeting at a party

TODD: Hi—you must be John's cousin Matt, **right?** From San Diego?

MATT: **Correct! I just got in** last night.

TODD: **I'm** Todd, John's roommate from Tech. **Glad to meet you. I can assure you that** I'm not anything like what John has told you.

MATT: **I'm happy to meet you, too**—and, yes—I have heard about you! Football player and **party animal extraordinaire**.

TODD: Football, yes—and **as a matter of fact**, I **do** like parties. **But tell me more about yourself** and **what you do** in San Diego.

MATT: Well, I'm more (of) a surfer than a football player. You know, San Diego has a fantastic coast—and we can surf all day and then party on the beach at night.

TODD: That sounds **awesome**. How long are you staying?

MATT: Well, I'll be here for two weeks. John has promised me a **nonstop schedule**— kind of **a mix** of sightseeing, meeting his friends, checking out **the local scene**, and—**hopefully**—camping in the mountains for **a couple of days**.

TODD: John's **a good guy**—and **you can be sure** he knows **the local scene**. He knows everybody in town. I'm sure he'll **show you a good time**. And his friends are here to help.

MATT: **Thanks so much**—I really appreciate that. I'm still a bit **jet-lagged** at the moment but should be **in good shape** by tomorrow. I'm **looking forward to** hearing what John **has in store** for me. . . .

TODD: Don't worry. We'll all take good care of you. And don't be surprised if we **show up on your doorstep** in San Diego one day, ready for surfing!

Improving your conversation

I'm Todd (Jones)

Simply using **I'm** and then saying your name is one way to introduce yourself. You could also say, for example, **My name's** Todd (Jones). It is customary to offer your right hand in a handshake to the other person. In very informal situations, you could just say Hi, **I'm** Todd, with no handshake.

To introduce one or more people other than yourself, say:

This is (my wife,) **Mary**. And **this is Susan, Bob**, and **Joe**.

To introduce more than one person and also tell how you know them, say:

These are my friends, **Susan and Bob.** And **this is Jim,** my coworker.

All of the people introduced would then shake hands. You could also say:

I want you to meet (my friends,) **Susan and Bob.**

Glad/happy to meet you

When you have been introduced to someone, it is customary to say **(I'm) glad/happy to <u>meet</u> you** or **It's nice to <u>meet</u> you.** The reply is **I'm happy to meet <u>you</u>** or **I'm happy to meet you, <u>too</u>.** (The underlined words are pronounced slightly louder than the others.)

Right?

Right? is an informal way to ask for confirmation that what you have just said is true. The answer can be **That's right!**

This train goes to Washington, **right?**	**That's right.**
You're from Panama, **right?**	**That's right,** I am.

Correct!

This is an informal answer to a question that asks for confirmation.

You're Matt, aren't you?	**Correct!**
This is Economics 101, **right?**	**Correct!**

If you want to tell your questioner that he or she is *not* correct, you can politely say this with, for example:

No, that's not **<u>right</u>**.
No, that's not **<u>correct</u>**.
No, I'm not <u>Matt</u>; I'm <u>Jim</u>.
No, she isn't my <u>sister</u>. She's my <u>cousin</u>.

(The underlined words in the examples should be spoken slightly louder than the other words in the sentence.)

To sarcastically indicate that something is *not* correct, **Yeah, right!** is used.

Dylan, I heard you just won the lottery jackpot!	**Yeah, right!** Where did you hear that nonsense?

Am, do, etc.

When a yes-or-no question using the verb *to be* is asked, the answer can be made emphatic by following it with a *tag*, in which, if the answer is *yes*, the verb is said a little louder than the other words. Affirmative tag answers are not contracted.

Are you unhappy?	Yes, I **<u>am</u>**.
Is he sick?	Yes, he **<u>is</u>**.
Are we winning?	Yes, we **<u>are</u>**.
Are they leaving?	Yes, they **<u>are</u>**.

When the answer is *no*, there are two ways to answer with a tag. The underlined words are the ones said a little louder. Negative tag answers are usually contracted. The full form makes them more emphatic.

Are you unhappy?	No, **I'm** <u>not</u>./No, I **am** <u>not</u>.
Is he sick?	No, **he's** <u>not</u>./No, he **isn't**./No, he **is** <u>not</u>.
Are we winning?	No, **we're** <u>not</u>./No, we **aren't**./No, we **are** <u>not</u>.
Are they leaving?	No, **they're** <u>not</u>./No, they **aren't**./No, they **are** <u>not</u>.

When an information question using any verb other than *to be* is asked, the answer can be made emphatic by following it with a tag, in which the verb is said a little louder than the other words.

Do you eat meat?	Yes, I **do**./No, I **don't**./No, I **do** <u>not</u>.
Does he like school?	Yes, he **does**./No, he **doesn't**./No, he **does** <u>not</u>.
Do we wait in line?	Yes, we **do**./No, we **don't**./No, we **do** <u>not</u>.
Do they live here?	Yes, they **do**./No, they **don't**./No, they **do** <u>not</u>.

As a matter of fact

As a matter of fact is a common expression that has a number of different meanings. In our example conversation it introduces a confirmation of what was previously said. It can go before the main clause or after the verb.

I heard you were looking for a job.	**As a matter of fact,** I <u>am</u>!
Your friend is very good-looking; is he single?	He <u>is</u>, **as a matter of fact**!

You can express the same meaning with **actually,** but put it after the verb.

I heard you were looking for a job.	I <u>am</u>, **actually**.
Your friend is beautiful, but I'll bet she's married.	She <u>is</u>, **actually**.

Just

This use of **just** indicates that something happened only a short time before. It can be used with the past tense or with the present perfect tense. For example:

Past tense	**Present perfect tense**
I **just** arrived.	I have **just** arrived.
They **just** finished.	They have **just** finished.
We **just** ate.	We have **just** eaten.
He **just** called.	He has **just** called.

To get in

To **get in** means to arrive and is usually used in the past tense.

What time did you **get in**?
They **got in** late last night.

Another way to say *to arrive*, when it refers to the future, is to **get there**.

I hope we **get there** on time.
She will **get there** by six.

To **get in** can also mean to be accepted by a school/college/university or other group with limited membership.

> He applied to that college and really hopes to **get in**.
> She didn't **get in** her first choice of sororities, but she **got in** another one, and she's happy.

I can assure you that . . . /you can be sure (that) . . .

These are common ways of saying that you believe something to be true, hoping to win the confidence of the person you are talking to.

> **I can assure you that** I will work hard.
> **You can be sure that** something interesting will happen.

Here is another way to express that you believe something to be true:

> **I promise you that** we won't leave until the work is done.

Party animal

Party animal is an informal expression used to characterize someone who spends a lot of time with friends or acquaintances for entertainment—either at home or in public places.

> My friend Eric will take you downtown on Saturday night; he's a real **party animal**, so you'll meet lots of people.

Extraordinaire

Extraordinaire is a word borrowed from French, pronounced in English "ek stra or d- NAYRE." It is used to exaggerate the meaning of the previous word.

> I'd like you to meet Marc—he's our pastry chef **extraordinaire**. You have to try his cheesecake!

What do you do?

The question **What do you do?** asks what one's job or occupation is. When you answer with a form of *to be*, you give a general job title. Note that the article *a* is always used when referring to only one person but is never used when referring to more than one person.

What do you do?	I'm a lawyer.
What does he do?	He's a painter.
What does she do?	She's a banker.
What do they do?	They're professors.

When the answer refers to someone who has a special title or position (i.e., is the only one in that position), use *the* instead of *a*.

What does he do?	He's the president of ABC Enterprises.
What do you do?	I'm the school secretary (the only one).

When you answer with another verb, you give more specific information about where you work.

What do you do?	I work for a large firm.
What does he do?	He drives a delivery truck.
What does she do?	She works at Atlas Bank.
What do they do?	They teach French at Loyola.

When a specific time or place is included in the question, the answer refers to how people spend their time, not just what their jobs are.

What do you do on weekends?   I relax and hang out with my friends.

What does she do at the beach?   She surfs, relaxes on the beach, and goes to the boardwalk for fun.

Tell me about yourself

Tell me about yourself is a polite way to let someone know that you are interested in learning more about him or her. It is better than asking direct questions, as the person being asked can decide what to tell and what not to tell. For example:

Tell me about yourself.   Well, I'm twenty-seven, I have a degree in mathematics, and I've been working at SYZ Company for three years. My parents are both economists, and I have a sister who's a nurse and two younger brothers. They all live in Connecticut, where I was born. I'm crazy about football and have season tickets. I listen to reggae, etc.

Tell me about yourself.   Well, I'm from a small town, and I came here to work.

Awesome

Awesome is an expression that is used a lot—maybe too much!—to say that you think something is really good. Other ways to express the same thing include **great**, **fantastic**, **terrific**, **wonderful**, and **cool**.

So . . . how do you like it here?   It's **awesome**!

Did you like the movie?   It was **awesome**!

Thank you for taking me— you're **awesome**!

Nonstop schedule

Nonstop schedule describes the activities of a very busy person, whether it be because of work, school, family responsibilities, or even social life.

I don't have time to see you this week, with my **nonstop schedule**.

Other ways to indicate nonstop activity are **around-the-clock** or **twenty-four-seven** (twenty-four hours a day, seven days a week).

I get telephone calls **around-the-clock**.

He works **twenty-four-seven**, so I hardly ever see him.

A mix

A **mix** refers to a combination of different elements, usually indicating variety.

There will be a good **mix** of music at the wedding, to keep the grandparents, the parents, and the young people happy.

We invited a **mix** of people—family, friends, coworkers, and neighbors.

Hopefully

Hopefully is a word inserted to indicate your wishes that something will happen. It can come in the middle of a verb phrase (will + **hopefully** + verb), before the subject, or at the end of a sentence.

> I'll **hopefully** graduate in two years.
> **Hopefully,** I'll graduate in two years.
> I'll graduate in two years, **hopefully**.
> If we leave right away, **hopefully** we'll arrive on time.

A couple of

A couple really means two; however, informally, it can mean more than that—but it does indicate a small number.

> I'll see you in **a couple of** hours.   I'll see you sometime today.
> It only costs **a couple of** dollars.   It costs less than five dollars.
> He'll be home in **a couple of** months.   He'll be home before the end of the year.

A good guy

Calling someone **a good guy** is a common way to recommend a male as being understanding of someone's situation, helpful, or generous. A female with the same kind of recommendation would be called **understanding/helpful/generous**.

> If you're looking for a used car, go see Sam Smith; he's **a good guy** and will probably give you a good price.
> If you want a teaching job, call Mary Johnson; she's very **understanding** and will give you good advice.

The local scene

The **local scene** refers to the culture and range of entertainment offered in a particular area.

> I'm moving to Springfield next month.   Oh, it's great! There are lots of things to do
> What's the **local scene** like there?   at night and on weekends.

To show someone a good time

To **show someone a good time** means to make sure he or she is entertained.

> If you come visit in December, we'll **show you a good time**. All our friends have parties in December!

Thanks so much

Thanks so much is a common way of expressing appreciation. Other ways to say this are **Thank you very much/Thanks a lot/I really appreciate this/You're a doll** (very informal)/**You're a sweetheart** (very informal).

The reply to any of these could be **You're welcome/No problem/I'm glad I could help you/Glad to help/Any time.**

> **Thanks so much** for fixing my tire.   **No problem.**
> **I really appreciate it.**
>
> **Thank you very much** for helping us.   **You're welcome. Any time.**

To be in good shape

To be **in good shape** means to be fit *financially* or *situationally*.

> My sister's husband has a good job, so they're **in good shape** financially.
> She has a good education and a lot of experience, so she's **in good shape** for the job market.

A similar expression, to be **in shape**, means to be *physically* fit.

> She exercises every day to stay **in shape**.
> You look great. How do you stay **in shape**?

To be looking forward to something

The expression **looking forward to** indicates that the speaker is very happy about a future event.

> I'm **looking forward to** seeing you on Saturday.
> She's really **looking forward to** going to college in the fall.

Another way to say this is with the expression, **can't wait to**.

> I **can't wait to** see you on Saturday.
> She **can't wait to** go to college in the fall.

To have in store for

The phrase **to have in store for** indicates an unknown situation that someone presents to someone else; it can be good or bad.

> Well, I'm going home, but I have no idea what my family will **have in store for** me.
> We're going shopping tomorrow to see what the designers **have in store for** us this season.
> He's been working there for years, but he never knows what's **in store for** him until he gets there.

To show up on someone's doorstep

To show up on someone's doorstep means to visit someone without notice. It doesn't necessarily mean that you plan to stay overnight—or longer—but it's possible.

> I was just getting ready to go out when my cousin **showed up on my doorstep**.

Related expressions are **drop in** and **drop by**, but these are used only for short visits—never an overnight stay.

> We were in town, so we decided to **drop in** to see you.
> Please **drop by** for a while. I miss seeing you.

To **show up**, on the other hand, is used negatively to indicate that someone often doesn't appear when expected.

> Pia said she was coming, but you never know if she'll **show up** or not.

Another meaning of **show up**, when used with a direct object, is to perform or seem better than someone else.

> Your singing was fantastic! You **showed up** all the other contestants.
> He will **show up** the competition with his fantastic speech.
> She **showed** us all **up** when she came in wearing that red dress!

Circle the most appropriate short answer for each question.

1. Is Larry coming tomorrow?
   a. Yes, he does.
   b. No, he doesn't.
   c. Yes, he is.
   d. No, he won't.

2. Do you like chocolate ice cream?
   a. No, I'm not.
   b. No, I don't.
   c. Yes, I am.
   d. Yes, she does.

3. Are we leaving at six?
   a. Yes, they are.
   b. Yes, they do.
   c. Yes, we are.
   d. No, we don't.

4. Is she a lawyer?
   a. No, she doesn't.
   b. Yes, he is.
   c. No, he doesn't.
   d. Yes, she is.

5. Are they here yet?
   a. No, they're not.
   b. Yes, they're.
   c. No, they do not.
   d. Yes, they do.

Match each remark in the first column with an appropriate response from the second column. Note: Some remarks have more than one appropriate response.

1. _____ Thank you!

2. _____ I just got in from Chicago.

3. _____ Are you a doctor?

4. _____ Tell me about yourself.

5. _____ I'm a real party animal.

6. _____ We're in good shape financially.

7. _____ You should go to college.

8. _____ You're a doll.

9. _____ Is this your doll?

10. _____ What does he do?

a. As a matter of fact, no.

b. Awesome.

c. Glad I could help you.

d. He's a cook.

e. I am, actually.

f. I hope I get in.

g. I'm a college student from Ohio.

h. No problem.

i. No, I'm not.

j. Then you can show us a good time.

k. Welcome.

l. Yeah, right!

m. Yes, it is.

n. You're welcome.

EXERCISE
1·3

Write a tag answer for each of the following questions.

1. Do you work twenty-four-seven?

   _____

2. Are you from New York?

   _____

3. Do your parents live in Los Angeles?

   _____

4. Are you a student?

   _____

5. Is your best friend studying English?

   _____

EXERCISE
1·4

Write a yes-or-no question for each of the following answers.

1. _____

   No, we don't.

2. _____

   Yes, she is.

3. _____

   No, they aren't.

4. _____

   Yes, I do.

5. _____

   Yes, he does.

6. _____

   No, I'm not.

Match the words or expressions in the first column with words or expressions in the second column that have a similar meaning. Note: There may be more than one match for each expression.

1. _____ a party animal
2. _____ extraordinaire
3. _____ awesome
4. _____ a mix
5. _____ you're welcome
6. _____ nonstop
7. _____ hopefully
8. _____ in shape
9. _____ a couple of
10. _____ a good guy
11. _____ any time
12. _____ the local scene
13. _____ look forward to
14. _____ have in store for
15. _____ show up
16. _____ get in
17. _____ can't wait

a. twenty-four-seven
b. a combination
c. an understanding male
d. arrive
e. attend
f. be accepted
g. current events here
h. fantastic
i. glad to help you
j. have plans for someone
k. if we are lucky
l. no problem
m. physically fit
n. round-the-clock
o. someone who likes to have fun
p. two
q. expert
r. want to

Circle the most appropriate response to each remark.

1. Are you Sam's brother?
   a. No, I don't.
   b. That's correct.
   c. I can assure you.
   d. As a matter of fact.

2. I'm the president's brother.
   a. Actually!
   b. You're a doll!
   c. Yeah, right!
   d. You're welcome.

3. We're leaving at six tomorrow morning.
   a. Awesome.
   b. I'm in shape.
   c. Any time.
   d. No, I'm not.

4. I work all the time.
   a. Yes, you're a party animal.
   b. Yes, you got in.
   c. Yes, you have just arrived.
   d. Yes, you're busy twenty-four-seven.

5. Are you coming to my party?
   a. I'm looking forward to it.
   b. It's a mix.
   c. I'm in shape.
   d. I can assure you that.

EXERCISE
1·7

Write a remark or question for each of the following responses.

1. _____

   She's a teacher.

2. _____

   You're welcome.

3. _____

   I can assure you that I'll show up on time.

4. _____

   I'm an engineer from Seattle, and I've been working here for six months.

5. _____

   I can't wait.

EXERCISE
1·8

Fill each blank with the correct form of the indicated verb.

1. I can't wait to (see) _____ you next week.

2. We are looking forward to (see) _____ you next week.

3. Are you looking forward to (go) _____ on your vacation?

4. What are you looking forward to (do) _____ there?

5. I can't wait to (hear) _____ all about it.

EXERCISE

1·9

Imagine you are introducing two of your friends to each other. Write what you would say and what each of your friends would say. Ask an English-speaking friend to check your answers.

_____

_____

_____

_____

_____

EXERCISE

1·10

Write a conversation between two people, using at least eight of the expressions explained in this chapter. Ask an English-speaking friend to check your answers.

_____

_____

_____

_____

_____

_____

_____

_____

_____

_____

Expressing opinions, likes, and dislikes

Conversation: Getting acquainted

LAUREN: Hi—you must be Sarah. I can **tell** from your picture. I'm Lauren. **Finally** we meet! **So** we're going to be **roomies** this semester!

SARAH: Yes, I recognize you from your photo, too! I'm so glad to meet you in person—and I see from your T-shirt that you **like** baseball. I'm a **big fan**, too!

LAUREN: Well, the T-shirt was a **going-away present** from my brother, who's a baseball player. Look on the back—it has a photo of all the players on his team. They **actually** won the city championship this summer.

SARAH: That's **awesome**. **I tell you**, I'm not very athletic, but I **love** to watch baseball, **even if** it's a **Little League** game. You **could say** I'm a professional spectator. What about you, do you play a sport?

LAUREN: Yes, I play tennis. **As a matter of fact**, I have a **scholarship**, and I'm going to play for the university. Now tell me, what else do you **like to do**?

SARAH: Well—what I **like** to do best is dance. I'm studying classical ballet, but I also **like to** dance to popular music.

LAUREN: **Cool.** We have a lot **in common**. I **like** to dance, too. Think you'll be **up for** checking out the local clubs this weekend?

SARAH: Oh, **yeah**. And the restaurants, too. **Speaking of which**—are you hungry? I'd **love** to **grab a bite** before it gets too late. I'm starving!

LAUREN: **Are you kidding me?** I'm always **up for** going out! How about trying the place up the street? I'm kind of hungry for a good hamburger.

Later:

SARAH: Lauren, **what do you think of** our room?

LAUREN: **To be honest with you**, I really **can't stand** that dark color on the walls. It's, **like**, really **depressing**. I prefer light colors. **Plus**, I'd **like** to change the rug and the bedspreads. Do you **like** them?

SARAH: No, I agree with you. They're **horrible**. With a couple of coats of paint and a few small changes, we'll make this room comfortable and cozy. Everybody will want to **hang out** here.

LAUREN: **Man**, I'm so relieved! I think we're really going to **get along**. I'm going to call my mom right now and tell her how **cool** my new **roomie** is.

Improving your conversation

Like

Like has a number of different meanings and uses. **What do you like?** asks what things a person finds pleasing.

Do you **like** ice cream?	Yes, I do./No, I don't.
What kind of ice cream do you **like**?	I **like** vanilla. My sister **likes** chocolate.

What do you **like to do**? asks what activities a person enjoys.

What do you **like to do** on weekends?	I **like to** relax and go out with friends.

Would you like . . . ? is a polite way of asking what someone wants.

What **would you like** for your birthday?	I **would like** a big party.
What **would you like** to do today?	I **would like** to go to the movies with you.

I'm/she's/he's/etc. like . . . is often inserted into a conversation to emphasize what someone is currently feeling or thinking. This is especially common among young people.

I'm **like** really mad at him.
She's **like** scared to death.
It's **like** the worst movie I've ever seen.

Love

Love, when it refers to a person or people, indicates deep affection. When love begins, there is often a feeling of great excitement, called **being in love**.

Her husband **loves** her, but she is no longer **in love with** him.

Love, when it refers to a thing, indicates a thing or an activity that a person finds very pleasing.

Do you like ice cream?	Yes, I **love** it!/No, I don't **like** it.
Do you like to go shopping?	Yes, I **love** it!/No, I don't **like** to.
Would you like to dance?	I'd **love** to!/I'm sorry; I promised someone else.

What do you think of . . . ?

What do you **think of** this? is a way of asking someone's opinion of something.

What do you **think of** the new teacher?	She's strict, but I **think** she's great. I **like** her.

Are you kidding me?

Are you kidding me? is an expression that indicates that something is so true—or untrue—that it doesn't need to be said.

Do you like to dance?	**Are you kidding me?** I'd rather dance than eat!
Would you like to go shopping tomorrow?	**Are you kidding me?** I have to study!

Up for

To be **up for** something means to want to do it.

Are you **up for** going to the movies with us?	Yes, I'd love to go.
I'm not really **up for** doing anything tonight. I'm too tired.	

Alternative expressions are to **feel like doing** something or to **be in the mood for** (doing) something.

Do you **feel like** going to a museum?	No, I'm not **in the mood for** (going to) a museum today.

Stand

To **stand** means to tolerate/to accept.

It's pretty hot today, but I can **stand** it.
He went home because he couldn't **stand** the hot sun.

Can't stand often means to not like.

He says he **can't stand** his little sister, but we know it's not true.

Big fan

To **(not)** be a **(big) fan** indicates that someone does or does not like something.

I like movies, but I'm not a **big fan** of science fiction.

Other ways of indicating something one likes include **awesome/cool/fantastic/great/amazing**.

College is **awesome**. My professors are **cool**, the classes are **fantastic**, the nightlife is **great**, and my friends are **amazing**.

These words are interchangeable—all of them work in the positions of the others.

College is **great/fantastic/cool/amazing**. My professors are **awesome/fantastic/amazing**, the classes are **awesome/cool/great/amazing**, the nightlife is **awesome/cool/fantastic/amazing**, and my friends are **awesome/cool/fantastic/great**.

Other ways of indicating dislike include **horrible/terrible/depressing/gross/disgusting**.

I didn't like that show; I thought it was **horrible**. The plot was **depressing**, and the dancing was **gross**.

Going-away present

A **going-away present** is a gift customarily given to someone who is leaving for an extended period, perhaps to go to college, to move to another area, or to work in another place.

They gave me a picture of everyone in the office as a **going-away present** when I left for my new job.

Tell

Tell is used in a number of expressions. It is followed by an object pronoun (*me/you/her/him/us/them*), the name of a person, or a word that refers to a person or people (friend(s), parent(s), etc.).

Tell me is a way of asking someone to relate information.

Call me and **tell me** about your classes.

After **tell me**, the subject-verb order of a question using the verb *be* is reversed.

Who **is she?**	**Tell me** who **she is.**
What **are you** doing?	**Tell me** what **you are** doing.

With all other verbs, the *do/does* is dropped, and the verb is conjugated normally.

What **do you do?**	**Tell me** what **you do.**
Where **do they go?**	**Tell me** where **they go.**
When **does he get in?**	**Tell me** when **he gets in.**

Don't tell me indicates that you fear a certain answer.

Don't tell me you're sick! (I'm afraid you're sick!)

I tell you indicates that you really mean what you are going to say.

I tell you, the dorm is really gross!
I'm telling you, it looks like rain.

Tell is used with *the truth*, with or without an object pronoun.

He always **tells** (me) the truth.

Can tell indicates the ability to know something without being told. It is followed by a new clause with a subject and verb.

I **can tell** (that) you had a good day by that smile on your face!
Can you **tell** I've been crying?

Say

Say indicates making an utterance but without indicating that it is directed at any particular person.

What did he **say?**   He **said** that he didn't know the answer.

Say to + an object pronoun or a person's name can be used to indicate information directed at a particular person or people.

What did he **say to you?**/What did he **tell** you?

You **could/might say** indicates a suggested conclusion.

You **could say** she's in love.
You **might say** the cafeteria food is gross.

Speak

To **speak** means to use a language orally.

They don't **speak** English at home.
She lost her front teeth and **speaks** with a lisp.
The teacher **spoke** for almost two hours.

Speaking of which is an expression that indicates that something mentioned reminds one of other information about it.

> I'm going to apply to the state university. **Speaking of which**, did you know Melissa is going there?
>
> Our state representative is up for reelection. **Speaking of which**, I heard she is coming to speak at our school next week.

Finally

Finally indicates relief that something long awaited has happened. It goes after a conjugated verb.

> I've been looking for my keys all day, and I've **finally** found them.

An expression with the same meaning is **at last**, which goes at the beginning or end of the clause.

> **At last** I've found them!
>
> I've found them **at last**!

So

So has many different uses. In the example conversation it introduces information that both people already know.

> **So** this is your new car. Will you take me for a ride?
>
> **So** you're getting married! Congratulations!

Actually/as a matter of fact

Actually and **as a matter of fact** often have the same function. They have many different uses. In the example conversation they indicate that a fact is a little surprising but of interest to the other person.

> So you're an Arabic teacher! I **actually** studied Arabic in college.
>
> I want you to meet my sister. **As a matter of fact**, she'll be here in a few minutes.

Even if

Even if can introduce a fact that seems a little hard to believe.

> I'm going to finish this paper **even if** I have to work on it all night.

Plus

Plus adds additional information that reinforces an opinion or argument.

> I like him. He's really nice. **Plus**, he's good-looking.

To be honest with you

The phrase **to be honest with you** introduces a statement that you think a person might not want to hear.

> Thank you for inviting me to the movies, but **to be honest with you**, I'm not really a big fan of horror movies.

Yeah

Yeah is an informal way of saying *yes*. It is pronounced with two syllables: "ye-uh."

Man

Man introduces something that the speaker feels strongly about. (It can be said to or by a male or a female.)

> **Man**, this course is really hard!
> **Man**, I wish I could take a week off!
> **Man**, your sister is beautiful!

Get along

Get along (with someone) means to live, work, or play with someone without problems or arguments.

> He's very easygoing. He **gets along** with everybody.
> Tom and his brother don't **get along**. They're always fighting.

Hang out

To **hang out** means to do something socially with one or more other people.

> We're going to **hang out** at Jess's house this afternoon. We'll probably just listen to music, maybe practice that new dance step.

Grab a bite

To **grab a bite** (to eat) means to get something to eat quickly.

> We're in a hurry to get there, so we'll just **grab a bite** to eat at a fast-food place.

Roomie

Roomie is an informal name for a person who shares a bedroom or home with you.

> How do you like your new **roomie**?

Scholarship

A **scholarship** is a prize or an award that provides money that enables someone to attend a private school or university.

> I'm hoping to get a **scholarship** so I can go away to college next year.

Little League

Little League is an organization that teaches baseball to children, organizes them into teams, and arranges games and tournaments for them.

> He just loves baseball. He's been playing it ever since he was in **Little League**.

Write a question using like *for each of the following answers.*

1. _____

   I'd love to have dinner with you.

2. _____

   No, I don't like fast-food restaurants.

3. _____

   We'd like to go to the mountains.

4. _____

   I like to go skiing then.

5. _____

   No, I'm not in the mood for doing that today.

6. _____

   Cherries are my favorite.

7. _____

   I don't know what he likes to do.

8. _____

   No. She prefers vanilla.

9. _____

   Yes, I love it!

10. _____

    Yes, I'd love to!

Fill in each blank with the correct form of say, speak, *or* tell, *as appropriate.*

1. It's important that you _____ the truth.

2. Her children _____ Spanish, Italian, and English.

3. Did you _____ him my secret?

4. What did he _____ to you?

5. What did he _____ you?

6. Can you _____ we've been fighting?

7. _____ what you think.

8. Please don't _____ that about us.

9. Please don't _____ my parents where we went.

10. Don't _____ me you missed the bus again!

11. I _____ you, that movie is great!

12. Mom called? What did she _____?

Change each question to a statement beginning with "Tell me . . . "

1. Where are you going?

   _____

2. What are they doing?

   _____

3. How do you get there?

   _____

4. When do you study?

   _____

5. Why is she crying?

   _____

6. What time do we leave?

   _____

7. Who are you texting?

   _____

8. How much does it cost?

   _____

Match the words or expressions in the first column with words or expressions in the second column that have a similar meaning. Note: There may be more than one match for each expression.

1. _____ great
2. _____ horrible
3. _____ can tell
4. _____ eat
5. _____ like a lot
6. _____ not argue
7. _____ not tolerate
8. _____ want to
9. _____ think of
10. _____ love

a. amazing
b. awesome
c. be a fan of
d. be in the mood for
e. be up for
f. can't stand
g. care about
h. cool
i. depressing
j. disgusting
k. fantastic
l. feel like
m. feel romantic about
n. get along with
o. grab a bite
p. gross
q. have an opinion about
r. know

Circle the word or expression that best completes each of the following sentences.

1. Why did you order this? You know I _____ this kind of food.
   a. don't get along with   c. can't stand
   b. grab a bite with   d. hang out with

2. She can afford to go to college. She has savings, _____ she got a scholarship.
   a. even if   c. yeah
   b. plus   d. finally

3. We are interested in buying the house we saw this afternoon. _____, it's much nicer than we expected.
   - a. Actually
   - b. Plus
   - c. Finally
   - d. Even if

4. Do you like your new roomie? Yeah, I _____ with her pretty well.
   - a. hang out
   - b. stand
   - c. am honest
   - d. get along

5. I just saw the movie that won the Academy Award for Best Picture. _____, what did you think of the dress the actress wore at the ceremonies?
   - a. Are you kidding me?
   - b. You might say
   - c. Speaking of which
   - d. I tell you

Circle the most appropriate response to each of the following questions or statements.

1. What did you think of her dress?
   - a. Are you kidding me? It was gross.
   - b. Man, I don't get along with it.
   - c. Actually, I'm not up for it.
   - d. I can tell you're honest with me.

2. Would you like to have dinner with me at the new Chinese restaurant?
   - a. Plus, my roomie's going.
   - b. Actually, I'm honest with you.
   - c. To be honest with you, I can't stand Chinese food.
   - d. You could grab a bite.

3. We're on the boat. Come over and hang out with us!
   - a. I'm up for that.
   - b. I tell you, it's depressing.
   - c. Speaking of which, I got the scholarship.
   - d. Plus, it's fantastic.

4. Man! I'm really hungry.
   - a. Let's join Little League.
   - b. Let's grab a bite to eat.
   - c. You could say we don't hang out there.
   - d. Speaking of which, I played in the Little League.

5. I've had a really bad day.
   - a. That's awesome.
   - b. Even if it's raining.
   - c. I can tell.
   - d. Even if you're tired.

Write an appropriate remark or question for each of the following responses. Ask an English-speaking friend to check your answers.

1. _____

    That's awesome.

2. _____

    Speaking of which, I played in the Little League.

3. _____

    I tell you, it's depressing.

4. _____

    I'm not in the mood for that.

5. _____

    As a matter of fact, I am.

6. _____

    You might say it's a little difficult.

7. _____

    Don't tell me you can't go!

8. _____

    Finally!

Write a conversation between two people in which they ask each other and tell each other what they like and what they like to do. Ask an English-speaking friend to check it for you.

_____

_____

_____

_____

_____

_____

_____

Answer the following questions. Ask an English-speaking friend to check your answers.

1. What do you like to do when you hang out with your friends?

   _____

2. What kind of restaurants do you like?

   _____

3. Are you usually up for going to your favorite restaurant, even if you're tired?

   _____

4. Where do you usually go to grab a bite to eat?

   _____

5. Is there anything you can't stand? Why?

   _____

Describing people, places, and things

Conversation: Talking about roommates

ERIC: **So**, Michael, what's your new roommate **like**?

MICHAEL: **Well**, if you have all day, **I'll** describe him for you. He's **quite the character**.

ERIC: I don't have all day, **dude**—but **basically**—do you get along with him?

MICHAEL: **Actually**, yeah—but that's only because we **hardly ever** see each other. The guy sleeps all day. Sometimes he gets up just to go to his classes, and **then** he comes back to the room and goes back to bed. **Then he'll** get up at midnight and study all night.

ERIC: **Really?** You don't eat together, **then**?

MICHAEL: **The truth is**, I don't even know when he eats, or where.

ERIC: **Then at least** he doesn't leave a mess in the kitchen.

MICHAEL: No! The guy is incredibly neat. He **actually** leaves the bathroom clean every day—and he doesn't seem to have dirty clothes. He's **like** a ghost.

ERIC: Man, I think you have the perfect roommate!

MICHAEL: **What about** yours? What's he **like**?

ERIC: **Well**, he's the exact opposite of yours. We're a lot **alike**, and we're together a lot. **I mean**, we have two classes together and we're in the same **fraternity**, so we're **really** good friends.

MICHAEL: **Sounds** to me **like** you have the ideal roommate!

ERIC: Well, yes—and no. Mine is a disaster in the house. **In the first place**, he always leaves a mess in the kitchen; he doesn't wash the dishes or take out the trash. **Plus**, he throws his clothes all over the place. **Not to mention** how he leaves the bathroom . . .

MICHAEL: **Come on**, Eric—he **sounds** a lot **like** you. **No wonder** you get along so well!

Improving your conversation

So

So has many different uses. In the example conversation, it is used to begin a question that is not surprising and may have even been expected.

> **So** how much do you want for the car? (You know I'm interested in buying it.)
> **So** when are we leaving? (We both know we are going somewhere together.)

Another use of **so** is to mean extremely.

> I can't wait to get there. I'm **so** excited.

To be like

Like asks for a description of a person, place, or thing.

> What's his wife **like**? Is she nice?   Yes, she's very nice.
> What's your new house **like**?   It's big, with four bedrooms and three baths.

To be **like** is also a slang (informal) expression that means to be thinking or telling your reaction.

> She comes home late, and **I'm like**, "Where have you been?"
> He told me I wasn't studying enough, and I **was like**, "What do you mean? I study for three hours every night!"
> The teacher told me I failed the math test, and I **was like**, "Oh man, my mom's going to be upset."

Look like, **smell like**, and **sound like** express similarity of appearance, smell, and sound.

> Mary **looks** (just/exactly) **like** her mother.
> This perfume **smells like** gardenias.
> When I talk to you on the phone, you **sound like** your dad.

These same combinations can also mean **seem like**, to indicate a guess about what is happening.

> It **looks like** (it's going to) rain.
> It **smells like** something's burning.
> It **sounds like** you're very upset.

When things are similar, they are said to **be**, **look**, **smell**, or **sound alike**.

> You guys **are** exactly **alike**—always getting into trouble.
> The twins **look alike**.
> These two roses **smell** (exactly) **alike**.
> You and your brother don't **sound** (at all) **alike**.

Will

Will—usually in contraction form (**'ll**)—is often used to make an offer to do something.

> **I'll** go to the store for you.
> **We'll** wash the dishes.

The same contraction can be used to emphasize that an activity is habitual.

> Sometimes when I'm alone I**'ll** go for a long walk.
> In the summer, he**'ll** stay up late every night playing poker with his friends.

Well

Well indicates that what you plan to say next may need a little explanation.

Did you write this letter?	**Well**, yes, but I was upset at the time, and I really didn't mean everything I wrote.
How are you?	**Well**, I'm OK now, but I've had a terrible week.

Dude

Dude is an informal, friendly way of calling a male friend or acquaintance instead of using his name.

> **Dude**, what time are we leaving tomorrow?

Basically

Basically indicates a summarized or generalized opinion.

What's your teacher like?	Well, **basically**, he's the worst teacher in the whole school.

Actually/the truth is

The terms **actually** and **the truth is** indicate that the speaker is telling the truth, even if it is surprising.

Do you like your new job?	**Actually**, yes—even though I work nine hours a day.

Another expression that means the same thing is **as a matter of fact**.

Are you moving?	**As a matter of fact**, I am!

Really

Really? is a way of asking if what was said was the truth.

I'm not going to study tonight.	**Really?** I thought you had a test tomorrow.

Really before an adjective means very.

> This movie is **really** good, but I'm **really** tired, so I'm going to bed.

Hardly ever

Hardly ever means almost never.

> You **hardly ever** call me anymore. Are you mad at me?

At least

At least indicates that a situation could be worse.

Ooh, it's so cold outside today! Well **at least** it isn't raining.

What about . . . ?

What about . . . ? is a way to ask the same question about a different topic.

Are you all going to the game? **What about** Joe?	Yeah, Jack and I are going. No, he can't go.

I mean

I mean precedes further explanation of the previous information.

She keeps her house really clean. **I mean**, she dusts and vacuums every day!

Other expressions that introduce further explanation include **in other words** and **that is**.

He studies twenty-four-seven. **In other words**, he's a serious student.
She's a real party animal. **That is**, she goes out every night.

In the first place

In the first place is used to present the first example of why you do or don't like something. **Second/in the second place** or **plus** can precede the next examples. A final example can be preceded by **not to mention that**.

We're not happy in the suburbs.
In the first place, it takes us almost two hours to get to work.
In the second place, when we get home, we're exhausted.
Plus, we spend so much on gas.
Not to mention that the kids are in day care for more than ten hours!

Then

Then can introduce a logical conclusion.

I've got my tickets, and my bags are packed.	**Then** you're all ready to go.

Come on

Come on is a way to say that someone is exaggerating a little bit.

I have to lose twenty pounds.	**Come on**, Alex, you're not that overweight!

It can also be used to ask for a reconsideration or change of mind.

I'm going to drive home.	**Come on**, dude, you've had too much to drink. Give me your keys!

Wonder

I wonder expresses an unanswered question or doubt. The subject-verb order is different from that of a question.

Where is Ellie?	**I wonder** where Ellie is.
Is Jon married?	**I wonder** if Jon's married.

No wonder indicates that something is obvious.

He's smart, energetic, well educated, and charming. **No wonder** you like him!

Quite the character

To be **quite the character** is to be unusual in some way.

She never stops talking but can always make you laugh.	Yeah, I hear she's **quite the character**.
He's really quiet and never talks to anybody, yet the girls all like him.	He must be **quite the character**.

Fraternity

A **fraternity** is an established social group of university men, who often live together in a **frat house** and mainly exist for social purposes. Fraternities are also known as **Greeks**, as they use Greek letters to form their names. Similar organizations exist for women and are called **sororities**.

EXERCISE
3·1

Circle the best answer for each question.

1. What are you like?
   a. I'm like, what's going on?
   b. I'm a little shy.
   c. I like chocolate.
   d. It's crazy.

2. What do you like?
   a. I'm like, who are you?
   b. I'm always busy.
   c. I like red dresses.
   d. I'm crazy.

3. Who do you look like?
   a. I look like my sister.
   b. It sounds crazy.
   c. I like my sister.
   d. I sing like my father.

4. What is your sister like?
   a. I like my sister.
   b. She likes to ski.
   c. She's tall.
   d. She likes me.

5. What is her boyfriend like?
   a. He likes her.
   b. She likes him.
   c. He's like, go home!
   d. He's very smart.

Write a question using like *for each of the following answers.*

1. _____

   He's very tall.

2. _____

   Yes, she does.

3. _____

   He's quite the character.

4. _____

   They like to play basketball.

5. _____

   She likes to play with dolls.

6. _____

   I'm honest.

Match the words or expressions in the first column with those in the second column that have a similar meaning. Note: There may be more than one match for each expression.

1. _____ in general   a. actually

2. _____ the truth is   b. as a matter of fact

3. _____ almost never   c. basically

4. _____ not to mention   d. hardly ever

5. _____ next   e. I mean

6. _____ it's no surprise that   f. I wonder

7. _____ very   g. I'm like

8. _____ in other words   h. no wonder

9. _____ I don't know   i. plus

10. _____ I'm thinking   j. really

                                       k. so

                                       l. then

Match each question in the first column with an appropriate response from the second column. Note: Some questions have more than one appropriate response.

1. _____ What is he like?

2. _____ What does he do?

3. _____ What does he like?

4. _____ Is he a singer?

5. _____ Does he play the piano?

6. _____ Is he in a fraternity?

7. _____ Does he call you a lot?

8. _____ When does he work?

a. Actually, he does.

b. Actually, he is.

c. Actually, he likes pizza.

d. Actually, he's really nice.

e. As a matter of fact, he doesn't.

f. As a matter of fact, he likes video games.

g. Hardly ever.

h. He doesn't have a job.

i. He looks like a movie star.

j. He's a carpenter.

k. He's a movie star.

l. He's awesome.

m. He's nice.

n. He's quite the character.

o. As a matter of fact, he is.

Circle the word or expression that best completes each of the following sentences.

1. Let's go home. I'm _____ tired.
   a. feel like
   b. basically
   c. really
   d. at least

2. We need another player for the team. _____ Tom?
   a. What about
   b. Actually
   c. As a matter of fact
   d. Hardly ever

3. It's a really hard course. _____, I'm up all night studying.
   a. What about
   b. Then
   c. Hardly ever
   d. I mean

4. She talks a lot. _____, she's on the telephone from the time she gets up 'til she goes to bed.
   a. So
   b. Then
   c. Plus
   d. Basically

5. This chair is _____ comfortable. I could sit here all day.
   a. so
   b. plus
   c. no wonder
   d. seems like

Circle the most appropriate response to each of the following questions or remarks.

1. Ben never showed up last night.
   a. Well, he hardly ever goes out.
   b. Come on, let's go out.
   c. At least he's sick.
   d. Actually, he's a party animal.

2. I don't think I'll go to the concert. It's too expensive.
   a. At least it costs $25.
   b. Come on, you have plenty of money.
   c. So you're going?
   d. I wonder if you have enough money.

3. What do you think of the new mayor?
   a. No wonder he is the mayor.
   b. I'll call him.
   c. What about Janice?
   d. At least he shows up at meetings.

4. There's a lot of traffic on Route 66.
   a. So where are we going?
   b. What about Route 95?
   c. Then we'll get there quickly.
   d. No wonder we like Route 66.

5. So, what do you like about your fraternity?
   a. In the first place, the guys are really cool.
   b. Dude, you're quite the character!
   c. I mean, she really likes her sorority.
   d. No wonder you're in a fraternity.

The following statements explain why a friend does not like her apartment. Write in the words or expressions (e.g., in the first place, not to mention that, in the second place, plus) *that introduce each statement.*

I do not like my apartment.

1. _____, it's in a terrible location.

2. _____, it's way too small.

3. _____, the kitchen has really old appliances.

4. _____, there's a leak in the roof!

EXERCISE
3·8

Complete the following sentences in your own words to explain why you like or don't like something. Ask an English-speaking friend to check your answers.

What do you like or not like? _____

In the first place, _____.

Second, _____.

Plus, _____.

Not to mention that _____.

EXERCISE
3·9

Write a conversation between you and a prospective roommate in which you describe yourself and ask him or her to do the same. Ask an English-speaking friend to check your answers.

_____

_____

_____

_____

_____

_____

_____

_____

_____

_____

_____

Striking up a conversation ◆·4·◆

Conversation: Running into a friend

NICOLE: Hi, Jen. **What's up?** I haven't seen you **for ages**.

JEN: Nicole! **Fancy running into you here**. Do you have time for a cup of coffee?

NICOLE: Sure. We really need to **catch up**. Do you work around here?

JEN: At the dress shop across the street. I'm a sales assistant **for the time being**, but I'm hoping they'll promote me to buyer after I have some experience **on the floor**.

NICOLE: Oh—I love that shop. Their clothes are so **trendy** and different from the **run of the mill**. You look fantastic—**I'll bet** their sales have gone up since you started working there.

JEN: Well—**I try! The thing is**, I enjoy the work, because I love the clothes, and I like helping people find what works for them. It's actually quite fulfilling.

NICOLE: Good for you. And I think the idea of becoming a buyer is great. **Before you know it**, you'll be working on your own designs. I remember how you **used to** dream of being a fashion designer.

JEN: Yeah, and I think this is **a step in the right direction**. Now, **what are you up to?** The last I heard, you were **about to** move across country. I hope you're back to stay!

NICOLE: As a matter of fact, I just got back a couple of months ago. I'm glad I went, because now I know I really want to be here. I'm working as a waitress right now but am hoping to get a teaching job. I've applied to most of the local school districts so **have my fingers crossed** I'll get something this fall.

JEN: What do you want to teach? I've heard **there are** openings for high school teachers in Howard County.

NICOLE: **No way!** I haven't even applied there. I'll do it **as soon as** I get home. Man, that'll be awesome if they need a biology teacher. Thanks for the **tip! Which reminds me**—waiting tables isn't all bad. On weekends I get pretty good **tips**. And **banking on** the info you just gave me, I think I'll follow you back to work and **splurge** on a new dress!

JEN: Great. I already have in mind some things for you to **try on**.

Later:

NICOLE: **Wow.** I love this one. I guess I'm **getting ahead of myself**, but I **have a feeling** this is just what I need for the interview with the principal.

JEN: And for the first day of school!

NICOLE: Thanks so much for your help. Now I'm really **pumped!** I'm so happy I **ran into** you today.

JEN: **Me, too.** Let's **make sure** we **get together** more often.

NICOLE: Yeah. I promise I'll **keep in touch**.

JEN: Take care, and **let me know** what happens. Bye for now.

NICOLE: Bye—and thanks again!

Improving your conversation

What's up?

What's up? is an informal way of asking people how they are. **What are you up to?** is a way to ask people what they have been doing lately.

Hey, Kim—**what's up?** — Oh, not much. How are you?
So, **what are you up to** these days? — Oh, just working, as usual. How about you?

Run into

Run into means to see someone by chance or in an unexpected place.

Fancy running into you here

Fancy running into you here means I didn't imagine I would see you. It is often said when you see people in places where you normally don't see them. Other expressions you could use in this situation are **fancy meeting you here** and **what a coincidence**.

For ages

For ages and **in ages** mean for a very long time.

How's Dan? I haven't seen him **for ages**. — Yes, it's been a long time. He's fine.

Before you know it

Before you know it means very quickly.

Oh, I'm so tired of school. — Calm down. **Before you know it**, you'll be finished and wishing you were back in school again!

As soon as

As soon as indicates that something will happen at the same time that something else happens.

We'll eat **as soon as** your dad gets home.
I'll call you **as soon as** I get the information.

Used to

Used to has several uses.
   To be used to (something) indicates a custom or habit.

At first it was difficult to live here, but now I **am used to** the cold weather.
I work the night shift, so I **am used to** staying up all night and sleeping during the day.

Used to (do) can indicate action that was once habitual but is no longer done, or a situation that was once true but no longer is.

She **used to** live next door to us.
He **used to** smoke.
I **used to** be married to him.

Used to (do) can also indicate an action that was done routinely in the past.

> When we were little, we **used to** swim in the lake.
> When he was a kid, he **used to** ride his bike to school.

This meaning can alternatively be expressed with **would (always)** or a past tense verb.

> When we were little, we **would always** swim in the lake.
> When we were little, we **swam** in the lake.
> When he was a kid, he **would always** ride his bike to school.
> When he was a kid, he **rode** his bike to school.

Try

Try on means to put clothing, shoes, or accessories on to see if they fit or if you like them.

> I would never buy shoes without **trying** them **on** first.
> **Try** this dress **on**. Let's see how it looks.

Try out means to use a car or other equipment to see how well you handle it or if you like it.

> Your new camera looks awesome!   Would you like to **try** it **out**?

Try to/try and indicate an effort to do something that may not be easy.

> **Try to** be here before eight o'clock./**Try and** be here before eight o'clock.

Try + verb in -ing form (something) indicates a suggestion for solving a problem or problematical situation.

> I can't get the door open.   **Try turning** the key in the other direction.

I try is a way to express modesty after receiving a compliment.

> You are a good cook!   Thank you; **I try**.

There is/there are

There is is followed by a singular or non-count noun to indicate that it exists.

> **There is** a stop sign on the corner.
> **There is** milk in the refrigerator.
> **There is** too much pollution here.

There are is followed by a plural noun to indicate that more than one person, place, thing, or abstract notion exists.

> **There are** a lot of bikes on the road.
> **There are** too many people in this class.

Wow

Wow is a common way to express surprise.

> Here is your exam.   **Wow!** I got an A.
> This is where we'll be living for a while.   **Wow**—it sure needs a lot of work!

I'll bet

I'll bet indicates sincere belief that what you are going to say is true, even though you have no proof.

What's Maria up to? **I'll bet** she's making a lot of money.

However, if you are replying to someone else's statement with **I'll bet**, this indicates that you do *not* believe it.

I hear Maria's making a lot of money.   **I'll bet.**

No way

No way is another expression that can mean two opposite things: definitely no or that's good news.

Are you going to Claudia's party?   **No way!** She hardly speaks to me.
We're going to the beach for a week.   **No way!** That sounds like a lot of fun!

On the . . .

To be **on the floor** means to be working as a salesperson in a store.

I'll bet you're tired after being **on the floor** all day.

To be **on the job** means to be working on a project that requires physical labor.

We're installing the electricity in   How long have you been **on the job**?
the new building up the street.

Trendy

Trendy is an adjective that describes the latest fashions.

It looks like long skirts are **trendy** again this year.

Run of the mill

Run of the mill is a way to describe something very ordinary or nondescript. If used before a noun, it has a hyphen between each word; if used without a noun, there are no hyphens.

My shoes are comfortable but not trendy. They are quite **run of the mill**.
This book is quite interesting. It's not just a **run-of-the-mill** romance novel.

Tip

A **tip** is an extra payment made to a server, taxi driver, beautician, barber, or anyone else working to provide a service.

The waiter gave us great service, so he got a good **tip**.

A **tip** can also be a helpful suggestion.

The teacher told us to answer the easy questions first. That was a good **tip**.

The thing is

The thing is introduces an explanation for a situation.

Why aren't you ready for school?	**The thing is**, I can't find my backpack.
How does that guy keep his job? He never does anything.	**The thing is**, he's a friend of the boss's sister.

A step in the right direction

A step in the right direction refers to an action that will lead to success.

I'm so glad you've decided to go to college. That's definitely **a step in the right direction**.

Be about to

To **be about to** means to be going to do at that moment.

I can't talk anymore. We're **about to** leave for the airport.
Fasten your seat belt. The plane is **about to** take off.

Which reminds me

Which reminds me introduces new information that is remembered because of something that was just said. An alternative to this expression is **speaking of which**.

I'm about to go shopping for Halloween costumes for the kids—**which reminds me**—do you still have the witch hat you borrowed from me last year?
I heard that Brittany was in town. **Speaking of which**, did you know she was getting married?

Have one's fingers crossed

To **have one's fingers crossed** means to indicate strong desire or hope that something happens.

I have my **fingers crossed** that we'll win the game tonight.

Pumped

To be **pumped** means to be very excited and ready for an occasion or event. An alternative expression is **all fired up**.

The whole team is really **pumped** about the game tomorrow. We're ready to win.

Bank on

To **bank on** means to rely on, count on, or trust certain information.

Do you think our candidate will win the election?	You can **bank on** it. All the polls say he's ahead.

Splurge

To **splurge** means to spend more money than necessary on something, because you really want it.

She got a bonus at work, so she **splurged** on a first-class ticket.
Why don't we **splurge** and buy the beautiful sofa instead of the run-of-the-mill one?

Another expression that indicates spending a lot of money is **go overboard**.

> It was their anniversary, so they **went overboard** and stayed at a five-star resort.

Get together

To **get together** means to meet.

> They **get together** every week to discuss their research.

Keep in touch

To **keep in touch** means to continue to contact each other.

> They have **kept in touch** for more than thirty years.

Catch up

To **catch up** can mean to find out the news of a friend you haven't seen in a while.

> Let's get together for lunch tomorrow. We have a lot to **catch up** on!

It can also mean to reach someone who is ahead of you.

> She's running so fast, we can never **catch up** with her.

Catch up can also mean to learn what the rest of the class learned when you weren't at school.

> After being home sick for a week, Adrian had to work hard to **catch up** on his lessons.

Get ahead of oneself

To **get ahead of oneself** means to make plans based on something that may not happen. Another expression that has the same meaning is **to count one's chickens before they hatch**.

> What? You just met him and you're already planning what to name your children? Aren't you **getting ahead of yourself**? You should never **count your chickens before they hatch**!

Have a feeling

To **have a feeling** about something is to think that it might be true or might happen.

> They've never met, but I **have a feeling** they might like each other.

Make sure

To **make sure** means to follow all of the steps that will lead to a desired outcome.

> Yes, you can take my car, but **make sure** you bring it back by four o'clock.

Let someone know

To **let someone know** means to tell a person information that he or she needs.

> I'm not sure I can pick you up. I'll **let you know** as soon as I find out if my car is fixed.

Me, too

Me, too is a way of saying that you agree with something positive that someone has said or that you have an activity in common with someone else.

> I really like living in Springfield.   **Me, too**.
> I'm going home now.   **Me, too**.

Me, neither is used to express the same meanings after a negative statement.

> I really don't like living in Springfield.   **Me, neither**.
> I'm not going home yet.   **Me, neither**.

EXERCISE 4·1

Choose between There is *and* There are *to complete the following sentences.*

1. _____ only twenty-eight days in February.

2. _____ a lot of people in this city.

3. _____ a big pothole in this street.

4. _____ too many cars on the road.

5. _____ too much traffic here.

EXERCISE 4·2

Fill in each blank with the correct form of the indicated verb.

1. We're not used to (live) _____ in such a small space.

2. We used to (live) _____ in a big house.

3. He's fine now, but he used to (get) _____ into trouble all the time.

4. She used to (smoke) _____. I'm so glad she quit.

5. I can't get used to (get) _____ up so early.

6. I used to (stay) _____ up late every night.

7. Are you used to (work) _____ this hard?

8. I know that guy. He used to (go) _____ to my school.

9. They are used to (be) _____ cold in January.

10. It's hard to get used to (drive) _____ in traffic.

Circle the word or words that best complete each of the following sentences.

1. Always _____ your best.
   a. try to do
   b. try doing
   c. trying on
   d. trying out

2. I love these shoes. I'm going to _____.
   a. try buying them
   b. try them out
   c. try them on
   d. try

3. Before you buy any machine you should first _____.
   a. try buying it
   b. try it on
   c. try it out
   d. try it

4. You're a very good driver! Thanks, _____.
   a. I try to.
   b. I try.
   c. Try me.
   d. I'm trying to.

5. I can't get my finger to stop bleeding. _____ a bandage on it.
   a. Try to put
   b. Try out
   c. Try on
   d. Try putting

Match the words or expressions in the first column with those in the second column that have a similar meaning. Note: There may be more than one match for each expression.

1. _____ What a coincidence.

2. _____ That's a wise decision.

3. _____ I'll bet.

4. _____ I agree.

5. _____ speaking of which

6. _____ hopefully

7. _____ count your chickens before they hatch

8. _____ soon

9. _____ for a long time

10. _____ I don't agree.

a. before you know it

b. Fancy meeting you here.

c. for ages

d. get ahead of yourself

e. I don't think so.

f. I have my fingers crossed.

g. Me, neither.

h. No way!

i. Me, too.

j. That's a step in the right direction.

k. What a surprise.

l. which reminds me

m. Wow!

Match the words or expressions in the first column with those in the second column that have a similar meaning. Note: There may be more than one match for each expression.

1. _____ be hopeful
2. _____ be all fired up
3. _____ be accustomed to
4. _____ see if something fits
5. _____ test something
6. _____ be working
7. _____ spend a lot
8. _____ meet
9. _____ write, call, or text
10. _____ make up missed work
11. _____ get news
12. _____ suspect
13. _____ not forget to do

a. be on the floor
b. be on the job
c. be pumped
d. be used to
e. catch up
f. get together
g. go overboard
h. have a feeling
i. have your fingers crossed
j. keep in touch
k. let someone know
l. make sure
m. splurge
n. try it on
o. try it out
p. run into

Circle the most appropriate response to each question or remark.

1. What are you up to?
   a. I'm not used to wearing a suit.
   b. I used to try.
   c. I'm pumped up.
   d. I'm about to go on vacation.

2. I'm going back to school.
   a. Me, neither.
   b. That's a step in the right direction.
   c. Don't get ahead of yourself.
   d. Thanks for the tip.

3. Be sure to talk to my friend. He's in charge of the program.
   a. Thanks for the tip!
   b. I'll try it out.
   c. I'll run into him.
   d. I'm on the job.

4. Fancy meeting you here.
   a. Yes, what a coincidence.   c. Yes, it's a fancy restaurant.
   b. I haven't seen him for ages.   d. It's a run-of-the-mill restaurant.

5. It was great to see you again.
   a. I'll catch up with you.   c. Try to catch up.
   b. Be sure to keep in touch.   d. You're getting ahead of yourself.

EXERCISE
4·7

Match each remark in the first column with all of the appropriate responses from the second column.

1. _____ That was great service.   a. I have my fingers crossed!

2. _____ What's up?   b. I try!

3. _____ This top is so trendy.   c. I'll catch up with him later.

4. _____ I have a feeling she's pregnant.   d. I'll keep in touch.

5. _____ Let's get together soon.   e. Let me know how it goes.

6. _____ I have a little extra money.   f. Let's splurge!

7. _____ You can get a coupon online.   g. No way!

8. _____ He's on the job now.   h. Not much.

9. _____ I'm pumped up about my date.   i. Thanks for the tip.

10. _____ Do you think he'll be there?   j. Try it on!

                                               k. Wow!

                                               l. I have a feeling he will.

EXERCISE
4·8

Supply the following information in complete sentences. Ask an English-speaking friend to check your answers.

1. Write three things you used to do but don't do anymore.

   _____

   _____

   _____

2. Write three things that you are used to doing now that you weren't used to doing some years ago.

_____

_____

_____

3. Do you keep in touch with an old friend? How?

_____

4. What do you and your friends do when you get together?

_____

5. What are you pumped up about?

_____

Write a paragraph of five sentences in which you tell what you try to do every day. Ask an English-speaking friend to check your answers.

_____

_____

_____

_____

_____

Write a conversation between two old friends who run into each other in a shopping mall—seeing each other for the first time in five years. Use at least eight of the expressions described in this chapter. Ask an English-speaking friend to check your answers.

_____

_____

_____

_____

_____

_____

Making dates and appointments

Conversation A: Making an appointment with a doctor

RECEPTIONIST: Drs. Manning and Sharp. How **can** I help you?

LISA: Hello. My name is Lisa Peterson. I'd like to make an appointment to see Dr. Sharp, hopefully sometime next week.

RECEPTIONIST: And what is it you want to see him about?

LISA: I need a complete physical for a new job I'm about to take.

RECEPTIONIST: Do you have a form that **has to** be filled out?

LISA: Yes, I do—and it looks like I'll need a pretty thorough exam.

RECEPTIONIST: **Can** you fax it to me? That way I'll know how much time to allot for your appointment.

LISA: Sure. **Can** you give me your fax number?

RECEPTIONIST: It's 202-739-5906.

LISA: Good. **I'll** fax it to you right away. **Will** you call me back when you get it?

RECEPTIONIST: **Right.**

Later:

RECEPTIONIST: Hello, Lisa. This is Dr. Sharp's office. I see you're going to need an hour-long appointment, and Dr. Sharp **won't be able** to do that for at least another month. **I could** give you an appointment with Dr. Manning next Thursday, **though**, **at** 1 p.m. **Would** you like to take that?

LISA: Um . . . yes, that sounds fine. Is there anything I **should** do to prepare for the exam?

RECEPTIONIST: Yes. I know this will be difficult, but you **mustn't** eat or drink anything after midnight the night before. **I wish I could** give you an appointment earlier in the day, but we don't have any other openings.

LISA: OK. But if there is a cancellation earlier in the day, please let me know. **I'd much rather** come in early in the morning.

RECEPTIONIST: **Of course.**

LISA: Thanks very much. Good-bye.

Conversation B: Changing a lunch date

LISA: Hi, Maria. It's Lisa. **Listen,** I'm not going to **be able** to have lunch with you next Thursday. I **have to** have a physical for my new job, and it's on Thursday at one o'clock—and it's in Alexandria. I'm really sorry. **Can** we make it another day?

MARIA: **No problem.** How about Friday **at** 12:30?

LISA: **Oh dear,** I **can't** do that, either. **Could** you do Wednesday?

MARIA: **Look,** we're going to have to make it the following week. We've **both** got **too much on our plates** right now. **Let's say** Thursday, the twenty-fourth, at one o'clock. OK?

LISA: **Perfect.** We'll have a lot to talk about by then!

Improving your conversation

In/on/at to indicate events

Events—dates, appointments, meetings, receptions, parties, concerts, classes, etc.—all have set days, times, and locations that are indicated by certain prepositions.

In indicates the month or year of an event.

> Her birthday dinner is **in** October.
> The celebration is **in** 2014.

On indicates the day or date of an event.

> The appointment is **on** Friday.
> Our classes are **on** Tuesdays and Thursdays.
> Her party is **on** August 13.

At indicates the time of an event.

> The reception is **at** ten o'clock.
> The concert is **at** 4:30.

Periods of the day are indicated as follows:

> **in** the morning
> **in** the afternoon
> **at** night

At indicates the location of an event or number in the street address.

> The movie is **at** the State Theater.
> The State Theater is **at** 405 S. Washington Street.

On indicates the name of the street in the address of the location.

> The movie is **at** the theater **on** State Street.

In indicates a location of an event where the address is already understood.

> The movie is **in** Theater A.
> The meeting is **in** the boss's office.

Modal auxiliaries

Following are explanations of the different uses of **modal auxiliaries**—verbs that modify other verbs in certain ways. They have the same conjugation in all forms.

I/you/he/she/it/we/they	**will/can/may/might/could/would/should/must**

Will can indicate a prediction for the future. The negative form of **will** is **won't**.

> We **will** get fat if we eat too much candy.
> He **won't** be here long—he's leaving in a few minutes.

Will + **probably** indicates what is likely to happen.

> I **will probably** be home after midnight.
> She **probably won't** be with me.

Will is used to ask and accept favors.

> **Will** you lend me your pen?   Yes, I **will**.

Won't is used to refuse to do something.

> **Will** you lend me a thousand dollars?   No, I **won't**.

Can indicates ability. The negative form of **can** is **can't**.

> Present tense: She **can** cook like a pro. She **can't** sing, though.
> Past tense: She **could** cook when she was very young. She **couldn't** sing then, either.

An alternative way to indicate ability is **be able** to.

> She **is able** to cook.
> She **was able** to cook when she was young.
> She **will be able** to cook like a pro when she finishes culinary school.

Can also indicates permission.

> Present tense: He **can't** go to the movies with us. (His mother said no.)
> Past tense: He **couldn't** go to the movies with us.
> Future: He **won't be able** to go to the movies with us.

May is another way to ask for and give permission.

> **May** we sit here?   Yes, you **may**./No, you **may not**.

May can also indicate possibility. Alternative ways to indicate this are **might** and **maybe** + **will**.

> It **may** rain tomorrow.
> It **might** rain tomorrow.
> **Maybe** it **will** rain tomorrow.

Could, in addition to being the past tense of **can**, also indicates a suggestion.

> How can I impress my boss?   You **could** wear a suit and tie to work.

Could is also a polite way to ask permission.

> **Could** I borrow a cup of sugar?   Of course, you **can/may**.

Should indicates direct or indirect advice.

> What **should** I wear to the interview?
> You **should** go home now.
> He **shouldn't** be here.
> Past tense: You **should have** gone home.

Ought to can be used to give direct or indirect advice. It is not used in a question or in negative form.

> What **should** I wear?   You **ought to** wear a suit.
> He **ought to** come to work on time.
> We **ought to have** been nicer to them.

Would is used with *if* to indicate how things could be different under different circumstances.

> If I were the teacher, I **would** make sure the children had fun while learning.

Would like is a polite way to say what you want.

> We **would like** three ice-cream cones.
> They **would like** donuts.

Would rather is a way to indicate preference. It is often contracted to **I'd, you'd, he'd, she'd, they'd.**

> She is teaching geometry, but she **would rather** teach algebra.
> I'm leaving now, but **I'd rather** stay here.

Would can also be a past tense marker, indicating repeated or habitual activity to describe the past.

> When we were little, we **would** go to my grandmother's house every Sunday for dinner.
> I **would** always play with my cousin, Bobby.
> Sometimes, we **would** get into trouble.

Must indicates probability. The negative form is not contracted for this meaning.

> He left at four o'clock, so he **must** be in Chicago by now.
> She doesn't answer her phone. She **must not** be home.

Must not indicates prohibition or strong advice. It is often contracted to **mustn't.**

> You **must not** put your feet on the table.
> You **mustn't** walk alone after dark.

Have to

Have to indicates obligation or necessity.

> Lee **has to** be at work by seven o'clock.
> Do you **have to** leave so early?   No, I **don't have to** leave. I thought you were
>   ready for everyone to go home.

Supposed to

Supposed to indicates advice to follow a custom.

> We're **supposed to** be seated at our desks before the bell rings.
> You're not **supposed to** text during class.

Wish

To **wish** means to be sorry that something is not true. It is followed by a verb in the subjunctive mood. Present tense subjunctive forms are as follows:

The verb *be*: use **were** for all subjects (I, you, he, she, it, we, they).

(You are not here.)	I **wish** you **were** here.
(We are not in California.)	We **wish** we **were** in California.
(He is not tall.)	He **wishes** he **were** tall.

All other verbs: use the past tense form.

(She can't go to the concert.)	She **wishes** she **could go** to the concert.
(I don't like to dance.)	I **wish** I **liked** to dance.
(She doesn't study enough.)	We **wish** she **studied** more.

I wish! indicates that it would please you if something said were really true, even though you believe that it isn't true.

You're the best student in the class.	**I wish!**

How about . . .?

How about . . .? is a way of making a suggestion.

I want to go shopping.	**How about** going with me this afternoon?
Do you have these shoes in size six?	No, but **how about** these? They're very similar.

Let's say

Let's say is a way of making a more forceful suggestion.

I want to go shopping.	**Let's say** you do your homework first.
Can you pick me up at 5 p.m.?	**Let's say** 5:30; I can't get there by 5.

Oh dear

Oh dear is an exclamation that indicates you wish something weren't true or hadn't happened.

> **Oh dear**, I dropped my bag and my stuff is everywhere.
> **Oh dear**, I said Friday and I meant Thursday. I'm so sorry.

Look

Look is an expression that indicates that you want the person you are speaking to to understand what you are going to say next.

You got here late!	**Look**, I said I was sorry.

Listen

Saying **listen** indicates that you want the person you are speaking to to pay attention to what you are going to say next.

> You won't believe what I just heard about Carrie.
>
> **Listen**, I don't want to hear any more gossip!

Both

Both is used as a pronoun or adjective to refer to any two people, places, objects, or abstract notions.

> I invited Todd and Carlos. I hope **both** of them can come.
> We went to New York and Washington. **Both** are fascinating cities./They are **both** fascinating cities./**Both** cities are fascinating.
> I couldn't decide which shoes to buy, so I bought **both** pairs.

Though

Though can be used to mean however—indicating that there is an alternative answer.

> Are you a good baseball player?
> Is he in the band?
>
> No, I'm good at hockey, **though**.
> No, he does play the guitar, **though**.

Have too much on one's plate

To have too much on one's plate is an expression that indicates that someone is very busy—probably because of an unusual project or happening.

> Look—I'd like to help you out, but we just moved to a new house, I'm learning a new job, and I just **have too much on my plate** right now.

Right

Right indicates that you understand or agree with what was just said.

> Am I supposed to wear a tie?
>
> **Right.**

Yeah, right! is a sarcastic answer that indicates that what was said previously is ridiculous.

> You're wearing a tie, of course.
> I got all As last semester.
>
> **Yeah, right!** [Of course not!]
> **Yeah, right!** [I don't believe you.]

Perfect

Perfect indicates that you accept a suggestion or offer.

> We can discuss this further at the meeting tomorrow.
> Shall we meet in the cafeteria for lunch?
>
> **Perfect.**
>
> **Perfect.**

Of course

Of course indicates that what was said is agreed to or obvious.

> Will you go over my homework with me?
> Do we have to work tomorrow?
>
> **Of course.**
> **Of course!** It's not a holiday.

No problem

No problem can mean that a request is accepted.

> Is it OK if I come in late tomorrow?   **No problem.**
> I have a doctor's appointment.

No problem can also be used as a reply to an expression of thanks. An alternative expression with the same meaning is **you're welcome**.

> Thanks so much for fixing my flat tire.   **No problem.**
> Excuse me, you dropped your wallet.   Oh, thank you!   **You're welcome.**

EXERCISE 5·1

Fill in each blank with the appropriate preposition (in, on, at).

1. The game is _____ Fairfax High School, _____ the gymnasium, _____ Saturday _____ eight o'clock _____ the evening.

2. Our wedding is _____ November _____ Springfield Country Club.

3. The inauguration is _____ 2013 _____ the Capitol _____ Washington, D.C.

4. The dinner is _____ Friday _____ six o'clock _____ the evening _____ Emily's restaurant _____ the back room.

5. The show is _____ July 24 _____ one o'clock _____ the afternoon _____ the art gallery _____ Jefferson Avenue _____ Leesville.

EXERCISE 5·2

Express the following using modal verbs or their alternatives.

1. (You are a student.) Ask your teacher for permission to leave the classroom.

   _____

2. (You are a teacher.) Tell your students that they are not allowed to leave the classroom.

   _____

3. Ask your friend if it is important for him to work today.

   _____

4. (You are the boss.) Tell your employee that she is obligated to work tomorrow.

   _____

5. (You are sick.) Ask your doctor for her advice about when to take the medicine she prescribed.

   _____

6. (You are a doctor.) Tell your patient that it is customary to take the medicine just before a meal.

_____

7. (You are a police officer.) Tell a pedestrian not to jaywalk (cross the street in the middle of a block).

_____

8. (You are a pedestrian.) Ask a police officer if it is necessary for you to wait for a green light before crossing.

_____

9. (You are a waiter.) Ask your customer if he prefers his steak medium or well done.

_____

10. Invite your friends to a party at your house on Saturday night.

_____

11. Ask your brother to pick you up at the airport.

_____

12. Tell your sister that you refuse to pick her up.

_____

EXERCISE
5·3

Match the words or expressions in the first column with the words or expressions in the second column that have a similar meaning. There may be more than one match for each item.

1. _____ she prefers   a. she can
2. _____ she wants   b. she cannot
3. _____ she is able to   c. she is supposed to
4. _____ she has permission to   d. she may
5. _____ maybe she will   e. she may not
6. _____ she is advised to   f. she might
7. _____ she probably isn't   g. she might not
8. _____ she probably doesn't   h. she must not be
9. _____ she accepts   i. she mustn't
10. _____ she refuses   j. she ought to
11. _____ she is advised not to   k. she should

12. _____ she is not allowed to

13. _____ she is unable to

14. _____ maybe she won't

l.   she shouldn't

m. she will

n.   she won't

o.   she would like

p.   she would rather

q.   she must not

EXERCISE
5·4

Fill in each blank with the correct form of the indicated verb.

1. I wish you (be) _____ here.

2. She wishes she (can) _____ go to school.

3. We wish they (will) _____ call us.

4. I wish we (have) _____ more time.

5. They wish I (do not) _____ spend my money on cars.

6. He wishes he (be) _____ back home.

7. Don't you wish it (be) _____ your birthday?

8. I wish I (can) _____ tell you the news.

9. I wish she (call) _____ me more often.

10. They wish she (live) _____ closer to their house.

EXERCISE
5·5

Write a sentence using I wish *to indicate your dissatisfaction with the statement.*

1. You don't love me.

   _____

2. My neighbors make a lot of noise.

   _____

3. My mother isn't here.

   _____

4. I'm not married.

_____

5. She can't stay here tonight.

_____

6. He won't move his car.

_____

7. She drives too fast.

_____

8. They come home late.

_____

9. I don't have enough money.

_____

10. Our house is too small.

_____

Circle the most appropriate response to each question or remark.

1. I wish we could take a vacation.
   a. Perfect.
   b. Yeah, right.
   c. Look—we can't afford it.
   d. Oh dear.

2. We'd rather go to the mountains than the beach.
   a. Listen—why don't you go to the mountains, and we'll go to the beach.
   b. Look—I'm tired.
   c. Perfect. Let's say we all go to the beach.
   d. Oh dear. Then we'll all go to the beach.

3. Can you help me with these packages?
   a. Oh dear, I can.
   b. Oh dear, I can't.
   c. Let's say no.
   d. Perfect.

4. Are you graduating in June?
   a. No problem!
   b. I wish!
   c. You have too much on your plate.
   d. I mustn't.

5. Why is your project late?
   a. No problem!
   b. Of course!
   c. I have too much on my plate!
   d. Right!

Match the words or expressions in the first column with those in the second column that have a similar meaning. There may be more than one match for each expression.

1. _____ Oh dear.

2. _____ Perfect.

3. _____ Of course.

4. _____ Let's say . . .

5. _____ Yeah, right.

6. _____ No problem.

7. _____ I wish.

8. _____ Look, . . .

9. _____ Listen, . . .

10. _____ Right.

a. How about . . .

b. I don't believe you.

c. I made a mistake.

d. It's OK with me.

e. No problem.

f. Of course not.

g. Pay attention.

h. That's a shame.

i. That's fine with me.

j. Too bad that's not true.

k. Understand this, . . .

l. Yes.

m. You don't need to ask.

Write a question or remark for each of the following responses. Ask an English-speaking friend to check your answers.

1. _____

Yeah, right.

2. _____

I wish!

3. _____

Of course!

4. _____

No problem.

5. _____

Right.

Write the details (name of event, day, date, time, location) of two events: one that you attended recently and one that you plan to attend in the near future. Ask an English-speaking friend to check your work.

Past event:

_____

_____

_____

Future event:

_____

_____

_____

Write a telephone conversation in which you make an appointment with a professional of some kind (doctor, lawyer, teacher, businessperson, etc.). Use at least eight of the expressions explained in this chapter. Ask an English-speaking friend to check your work.

_____

_____

_____

_____

_____

_____

_____

_____

_____

_____

_____

Expressing wants and needs

Conversation: Looking for a new apartment

RECEPTIONIST: Good morning! How can I help you?

TED: **I'd like** to rent an apartment in this neighborhood and wonder if you can help me.

RECEPTIONIST: You **need** to talk to Shirley—she's our **go-to** agent for apartment rentals. Here, I'll take you to her office.

SHIRLEY: Hello, I'm Shirley. Have a seat and tell me what kind of apartment you're looking for. Is it just for you?

TED: Well, that depends on what's available. I'd really rather live alone, but if I don't see anything that works, I could share a bigger place with a friend of mine.

SHIRLEY: OK. First, tell me what you **have in mind**.

TED: The most important thing is the location. I want to be in the city, **preferably** in this neighborhood, so I can walk to the university and to the metro station. I don't have a car.

SHIRLEY: OK, then you **don't mind** if there's no parking space.

TED: Exactly. But I want a secure building. I also want it to have a living room, a dining room, one bedroom, and, of course, a modern kitchen and bathroom. I don't really **need all the bells and whistles**, but I would like to have a balcony.

SHIRLEY: And what is your budget? I mean, what monthly rent are you thinking about, including **utilities**?

TED: I'm hoping to find something for about $700 a month.

SHIRLEY: Look, I can tell you right now **there are no** decent apartments in this area under $1,200 a month—and **none** of them **have** dining rooms or balconies. There are modern, secure buildings that are actually near the metro—but they're at least six miles outside of the city.

TED There's no way I'm going to live way out there. Do you think you could find a two-bedroom place closer in for, **say**, $1,400 a month? Something I could share with my friend?

SHIRLEY: Let me do a little research this morning and see what I can find. I'm not going to tell you that it's impossible, but I can't promise anything, either. Give me a couple of hours to see what's **out there**. If I find anything **worthwhile**, we can go **have a look** this afternoon. **In the meantime**, I **need** you to fill out this form so I have your contact information. As a matter of fact, both you and your friend will have to fill out an application in order to be approved as tenants. I'm assuming you want a one-year lease. Is that right? Oh, **one more thing**: you don't have a pet, do you?

TED: Yes, I'm willing to sign a one-year lease, and no, I don't have a pet. And I'll make sure my friend **gets rid of** his dog. He can leave it with his family—they have a place in the **country**. I'd better go give him a **heads-up** right now.

SHIRLEY: Good. Be sure both of you bring your financial and credit information with you.

TED: Right. We'll see you at noon, then. Thank you very much.

SHIRLEY: See you later.

Improving your conversation

Need

There are several words that indicate that something is required. To **need** is used to require urgent attention or action to prevent damage.

> I **need** a doctor. I'm really dizzy.
> We **need** to rest. We've been working for six hours.
> Flowers **need** water.

Need can also indicate a requirement dictated by someone else.

> I **need** six more credits in order to graduate.
> The children **need** to bring pencils and erasers to class.
> To be a taxi driver, you **need** to have a special driver's license.

To **have to** can indicate a personal need or an obligation to someone else.

> I **have to** get my car fixed.
> He **has to** work on Saturdays.
> You **have to** complete the prerequisites before you can take advanced courses.
> She was speeding and **has to** pay a $100 fine.

To be required to indicates you have to do something that is imposed by some sort of authority.

> The children are **required to** do their homework before watching television.
> The cadets are **required to** wear their uniforms to class.
> This warrant means you are **required to** allow the police to search your office.

A **requirement** is a standard imposed on someone by some sort of authority.

> Ability to speak another language is a **requirement** for this position.
> It's a **requirement** of the home owners' association that you keep your yard neat.

A **prerequisite** is proof of previous instruction or ability necessary for a certain job, course, or position.

> This course is open to beginners. There are no **prerequisites**.
> A master's degree in business is a **prerequisite** for this job.

Want

To **want** means to have a desire for something and indicates some belief that it will be attained.

> We **want** to move to a better neighborhood. (We're saving our money.)
> She **wants** to go to college. (She is trying to make good grades in high school.)
> He **wants** an ice-cream cone. (He is going to the ice-cream store/ordering ice cream.)

Would like indicates a desire that may or may not be possible to satisfy.

> **We'd like** a house with four bedrooms.
> **I'd like** to go on a vacation.
> **He'd like** to be able to visit his family at least once a year.

Mind

To **have in mind** means to have a good idea of the kind of thing you want.

> Sure, I'll help you decorate your living room. What kind of look do you **have in mind**?

To **have a mind to** means to be strongly considering an action.

> He stole money from me! I **have a mind to** report him.

To **mind** can mean to not be happy about something. This is the meaning used in the example conversation.

> I don't **mind** going to the store. I'm happy to do it.

To **mind** can mean to take charge of a store or shop.

> Thank you for **minding** the store while I had lunch.

To **mind** can also mean to babysit.

> Could you **mind** the children while I go to the store?

To **mind** can also mean to pay attention to.

> No, I won't babysit for your children, because they won't **mind** me.
> Don't **mind** her—she doesn't know what she's talking about.

To **make up your mind** means to decide.

> Do you want pizza or pasta? **Make up your mind!**
> I can't **make up my mind** between the SUV and the van.

To **change your mind** means to have a different idea or opinion than before.

> I was going to paint the dining room red, but I **changed my mind** and painted it blue.

Never mind means to disregard what was said. **Forget it** is another way of expressing this.

> What did you say?   **Never mind**—it wasn't important.

Mind is also a noun that refers to the brain.

> At the age of ninety-five, her body is weak, but her **mind** is still perfect.

A **mind reader** is someone who knows what someone else is thinking.

> How was I supposed to know you had a headache? I'm not a **mind reader**.

There is and there are

There is indicates that something exists, and is followed by a singular noun.

> **There is** a gas station up ahead.

There are indicates that more than one thing exists, and is followed by a plural noun.

> **There are** several gas stations about three miles down the road.

Words that indicate that nothing exists—such as **zero**, **no**, and **not any**—are followed by a plural noun.

> We have exactly **zero** applications for the position.
> There are **no** heart specialists in this area.
> She does**n't** have **any** brothers or sisters.

Likewise, the pronoun that takes the place of these words, **none**, is followed by a plural verb.

> We have three teachers to contact, but **none** (of them) **are** available this week.

Have a look

To **have a look** means to make a short investigation.

> I lost my earring yesterday. Do you think it might be at your house?   I'll **have a look** and see if I can find it.

Get rid of

To **get rid of** means to make sure to no longer have something.

> The car used too much gas, so we **got rid of** it. We sold it last week.
> You should **get rid of** that suit. It doesn't look good on you.

Preferably

Preferably indicates someone's first choice.

> I'd like to buy a new car, **preferably** one that doesn't use much gas.

Go-to

Go-to is an expression used as an adjective to describe a person, place, or object that people depend on or "go to first" for what they need.

> You need a handyman? Call Ron—he's my **go-to** person for everything that goes wrong in the house.
> I love Cherrydale Hardware. It's my **go-to** store for supplies.

Worthwhile

Worthwhile describes something that has value in terms of time, money, experience, or purpose.

> The translation course is intensive, but it is really **worthwhile**.
> Cancer research is a **worthwhile** cause.

Out there

Out there is an expression that refers to the real world, at the present time.

> Go out and have fun! There are a lot of nice people **out there**.
> I'm always careful walking at night. You never know what dangers are **out there**.

Utilities

Utilities include the services necessary for the functioning of a house or apartment, including those for water and sewage, heating, air-conditioning, electricity, and sometimes trash collection.

Some apartment buildings include the cost of **utilities** in the monthly rent, and some don't.

All the bells and whistles

The expression **all the bells and whistles** refers to the most modern, up-to-date—usually expensive—features of homes and other buildings that are either new or recently remodeled.

The apartment has **all the bells and whistles**—a soaking tub with jets, multiple showerheads, granite countertops and stainless-steel appliances in the kitchen, energy-efficient appliances, and many more exclusive features.

Country

Country can refer to a nation.

What **country** are you from?   I'm from Colombia.

Country can also refer to the areas that are distant from cities, often where there are farms.

We like to go to the **country** on weekends, to get some peace and quiet.

A heads-up

A heads-up is a warning that something is going to happen, so that the other person will be ready.

Hey, Mom—I'm bringing a friend home for dinner and wanted to give you **a heads-up**.

Say

Say can introduce an example of a possibility.

I'm sure you can get someone to pick you up. Why don't you ask, **say**, Rosita or Laura?
Why don't you paint this room a brighter color, **say**, yellow or green?

In the meantime

In the meantime indicates a period of time between two events. Another word with the same meaning is **meanwhile**.

It will be a big help if you go to the store and get what we need for dinner. **In the meantime**, I'll set the table.
Joey had to go away for six months. **In the meantime**, Julie went to classes and learned to cook.

One more thing

One more thing is an expression used at the end of a series of remarks. It could be something important that you almost forgot to say or a question that you almost forgot to ask.

OK, now, go to school. Mind the teacher, try to finish all your work, and don't pick fights with the other kids. **One more thing:** don't forget to thank the teacher for helping you with your math!
So, doctor, I'll take the medicine you gave me and go to physical therapy. **One more thing**—when do you think I'll be able to go back to work?

Fill in each blank with an appropriate word or expression from this chapter.

1. Get up! We _____ be at the airport by eight o'clock.

2. Do you _____ anything from the drugstore?

3. I'm working hard because I _____ to save money to buy a house.

4. Are there any _____ for this course?

5. Waiter, we _____ to order our meal now.

6. He fell down the stairs! He _____ an ambulance.

7. Please, _____ turning the music down?

8. In the military, you are _____ obey orders.

9. Writing a ten-page paper is one of the _____ of this course.

10. What do I _____ do to get a license?

Match the words or expressions in the first column with those in the second column that have a similar meaning. There may be more than one match for each expression.

1. _____ have to

2. _____ want to

3. _____ never mind

4. _____ not care

5. _____ not be bothered

6. _____ have a new opinion

7. _____ be intelligent

8. _____ mind

9. _____ decide

a. babysit

b. be in charge of the store

c. be required to

d. change your mind

e. forget it

f. have a good mind

g. have a mind to

h. need to

i. not mind

j. pay attention to

k. would like to

l. wouldn't mind

m. make up your mind

EXERCISE
6·3

Circle the most appropriate response to each question or remark.

1. There are no decent men for me to date.
   a. Come on! There are lots of worthwhile men out there.
   b. Give me a heads-up.
   c. Make up your mind.
   d. Never mind. He's our go-to person.

2. The utilities will cost us a fortune.
   a. It's a prerequisite.
   b. Have a look at the basement.
   c. Still, the house is worthwhile.
   d. It's out there.

3. Why don't you consider a trip to, say, the Caribbean or Hawaii?
   a. It's not a requirement.
   b. One more thing, it's in the country.
   c. I need a heads-up.
   d. I wouldn't mind that.

4. He's our go-to mechanic.
   a. I need to talk to him.
   b. Get rid of the car.
   c. I have a mind to drive home.
   d. This is worthwhile.

5. This house has all the bells and whistles.
   a. I don't see any bells.
   b. It's out there.
   c. I'll mind them.
   d. But it's in the country.

EXERCISE
6·4

Write a question or remark for each of the following responses. Ask an English-speaking friend to check your work.

1. _____

   Give me a heads-up.

2. _____

   It's definitely worthwhile.

3. _____

   Preferably, in the country.

4. _____

   Let's have a look.

5. _____

   We wouldn't mind.

6. _____

I've changed my mind.

7. _____

How about, say, a ring or a necklace?

8. _____

None of them are here.

9. _____

She's our go-to travel agent.

10. _____

Get rid of it.

Write a word or expression from this chapter for each definition.

1. to babysit

   _____

2. to investigate

   _____

3. to feel like doing

   _____

4. zero

   _____

5. to throw out

   _____

6. to warn

   _____

7. to have value

   _____

8. between now and then

   _____

9. to have a new opinion

   _____

10. heat, electricity, water

_____

11. Oh, I almost forgot . . .

_____

12. not the city

_____

13. trusted source

_____

14. for example

_____

15. forget it

_____

16. the brain

_____

17. obligatory

_____

18. requirement for beginning

_____

19. modern features

_____

20. in today's world

_____

EXERCISE
6·6

Answer the following questions in complete sentences. Ask an English-speaking friend to check your answers.

1. What do you want to accomplish in the next five years?

_____

_____

_____

2. What do you need to do to reach your goals?

_____

_____

_____

3. What are you required to do at work/at school/at home?

_____

_____

_____

4. What do you have to do this week?

_____

_____

_____

5. What would you like to do this weekend?

_____

_____

_____

6. What chores do you not mind doing?

_____

_____

_____

Making requests and offers

Conversation: Helping a classmate

JIM: Hey, buddy, can I ask you a **favor**?

ALI: Sure—what can I do for you?

JIM: I wonder if you'd **be willing** to lend me your biology notes. I **missed** a couple of classes when I was sick, and now I'm **totally** lost.

ALI: OK. Why don't we go to the library and copy my notebook and then **go to** your place and **go over** the lessons. I'm **acing** biology this semester, so I'm sure I can get you **back on track**.

Later:

JIM: Oh, man, that will be **a load off my shoulders**. I can't thank you enough.

ALI: Glad to help. As a matter of fact, I have a favor to ask of you.

JIM: **Oh yeah?** Don't tell me you need more advice about your girlfriend!

ALI: Well, not exactly. **It's that** her sister is coming up for the weekend, and I need to find her a **date**. **Any chance** you'd go out with her on Saturday night? We'd all four go to the theater and then out to eat.

JIM: Look, I already agreed to go to the movies with Ben. But **how about if** I invite her to go to the movies with us **instead**? Of course, afterward we'd grab a bite to eat, but it won't be anything **fancy**.

ALI: That sounds great to me. Let me see what Jessica thinks about it, and I'll **get back to you ASAP**.

JIM: Good. And **by the way**, thanks again for the help with biology. I think I'm **on top of it** now.

ALI: No problem. **Don't hesitate** to call me if you have any questions.

JIM: Thanks, buddy. **See you later**.

Improving your conversation

Making requests

A direct command is the strongest way to request urgent attention.

> **Take** her to the hospital!
> **Let** us rest!
> **Call** the police!
> **Help** me!

Can you can also be used to request attention to a need.

> **Can you** get me to a hospital right away?
> **Can you** call the police?
> **Can you** help me?

A direct command for assistance in attaining something you want (rather than something you need) is considered rude. **Can you** is also a little abrupt.

Will you is the most direct way to request what you want and should always be preceded or followed by **please**.

> **Will you please** take me to the airport?
> **Please, will you** bring me a glass of water?

Could you (please) is a more polite way to request what you want.

> **Could you** babysit for my daughter this weekend?
> **Could you** tell us how to get to Main Street from here?

Would you (please) is an even more polite way to request what you want.

> **Would you** (be able to) mow the lawn for me this weekend?
> **Would you** take me to the store this afternoon?

Would you mind + -ing is the most formal way to ask someone to do something for you.

> **Would you mind** help**ing** me with these packages?
> **Would you mind** tell**ing** us how to get to the main highway?

Would you mind if + subjunctive is a very polite way to ask permission to do something.

> **Would you mind** if I borrow**ed** your car?   No, you can use it for a couple of hours.
> **Would you mind** if we stay**ed** one
>   more night?

To **mind** can mean not be happy about.

> Do you **mind** if I use your pen?   No, I don't **mind**.
> Do you **mind** if I borrow your car?   Yes, I do **mind**! You may not borrow it.

A **favor** is something that someone does to help someone else out.

> Will you do me a **favor**?   Of course. What do you need?
> Would you mind if I asked you a **favor**?   Of course not. What can I do for you?

Offering assistance

Several expressions are used to offer a favor or assistance.

I'll + verb indicates that you are taking action in an emergency. An alternative way to express this is to use the present progressive tense.

> **I'll take** you to the hospital.
> **I'm calling** the police.

Would you like to + basic verb or **would you like me to + basic verb** can be used when what the person needs is obvious but not urgent.

> I see you're tired. **Would you like to** sit down?
> I see you need a ride. **Would you like me to** take you home?

Let me know if I can help you or **I'll be glad to help you** are formal expressions used by receptionists, secretaries, salesclerks, or other people whose jobs involve providing services to the public.

> The doctor will be with you shortly. In the meantime, **let me know if I can help you**.
> Feel free to look through our merchandise, and if you see anything you like or have any questions, **I'll be glad to help you**.

Can I help you? is a way to offer assistance to a stranger in need. An alternative expression is **Let me help you.**

> You look lost. **Can I help you?**
> You took quite a fall. **Let me help you** get up.

How can I help you? is a way to offer assistance to someone who seems to want something. An alternative expression is **What can I do for you?**

> I'm the doctor's receptionist. **How can I help you?**
> I see you're waiting for a salesperson. **What can I do for you?**

Is there any way I can help you? indicates a sincere offer of help to someone you know well. Alternative expressions are **Is there anything I can do for you?/Is there anything I can do to help?**

> Mom, I know you're not feeling well. **Is there any way I can help you?**
> So you're moving to your new house next week! **Is there anything I can do to help?**

Oh yeah

The expression **oh yeah** can have different meanings, depending on the intonation. In the example conversation, with ascending intonation (from low to high), it affirms interest in what was just said. Following is another example:

> I'm leaving for San Francisco tomorrow morning.
> **Oh yeah?** What are you going to do there? How long are you staying?

When **oh yeah** has descending intonation (from high to low), it affirms previous knowledge of what was just said.

> C'mon, let's eat lunch.
> I thought you were having lunch with Tim.
> **Oh yeah**, I forgot about that.

It's (just) that . . .

It's (just) that . . . is an expression that precedes an explanation of something just mentioned or questioned. It indicates that the speaker expects the hearer to understand and accept the explanation.

> Why didn't you turn your paper in on time?
> I'm sorry, professor. **It's that** I had two exams and three other papers due last week.

Another way to express this is **the thing is, . . .**

> Why don't you ever wash your dishes?
> **The thing is**, I always seem to be in a hurry to go somewhere.

Date

A **date** is an appointment with someone—often for the prospect of a romantic connection—for a social occasion.

> I'd really like to go to dinner with you on Friday, Rita, but I have a **date** with that new guy at work. He invited me to go to the movies with him.

Totally

Totally means completely, 100 percent, very.

> Oh, the party was **totally** awesome.
> We were **totally** confused by his explanation.

Be willing

To **be willing** means to accept participation in an activity.

> Are you **willing** to pick me up at the airport?
>
> Sure, what time does your plane land?
>
> He can move to Los Angeles if he wants to, but I'm not **willing** to quit my job and go with him.

Back on track

To be **back on track** means to be back to normal after a difficult period.

> Tran missed three practices after he sprained his ankle, but he's been doing extra training, and now he's **back on track** with the rest of the team.
> The divorce was hard, but Phil is now getting his life **back on track**.

On top of it

To be **on top of it** means to fully understand something or to be able to handle something.

> The math course is hard, but I think he's **on top of it**.
> There was a lot to learn in my new job, but now I'm **on top of it**.

A load off my shoulders/mind

A load off my shoulders/mind is a big relief from responsibility or worry.

> When Jan offered to take care of my mother, it was a huge **load off my shoulders**.
> The other driver admitted that the accident was his fault, and his insurance company paid for my car repairs. That sure was **a load off my mind**.

Miss

To **miss** can mean to not be able to attend an event or participate in normal activities.

> I'm sorry I **missed** your party. I was out of town.
>
> Yeah, and you **missed** the chance to meet my cousin from St. Louis.

He **missed** a week of work when he was sick.
You played the wrong card. Now you have to **miss** your turn.

Miss can also mean to arrive too late for a form of public transportation.

We got stuck in traffic and **missed** our plane. Now we have to reschedule.

Miss can also mean to feel nostalgic or sad about a person you haven't seen, a place you haven't been to, or an activity you haven't participated in for a while.

I **miss** you, I **miss** Arlington, and I **miss** hanging out with you guys.

Miss can also mean failure to answer a question correctly on a test or to connect with a ball (or other object) in a game.

She **missed** six questions on the test and failed it.
You'd better get your eyes checked—you **missed** the ball three times!

Go and come

To **go** means to move *from here or there to another place.*

I'm **going** to the airport tonight.
When are you **going** to Colorado?

To **come** can mean to move *from there to here.*

(I am at work now.) I'm **coming** to work early tomorrow.
(I am in Colorado.) When are you **coming** to Colorado?

To **come** can also mean to move *from here to there*—when the person you are talking to is expected to be *there.*

(I am at work now; you are at home.) I'm **coming** home early this afternoon.
(I am in Virginia; you are in Colorado.) I'm **coming** to Colorado in August.
(We are both at the office.) I hope you can **come** to the party at my house next week.

To **go over** can emphasize that the movement *from here to there* or *to another place* is short.

Go over to your neighbor's house and see if she is at home.

To **go over** can also mean to read or review something in order to understand or remember it better.

I'm going to **go over** my notes tonight. We have a big test tomorrow.

To **come over** emphasizes that the movement *toward you or toward the person you are speaking to* is short.

I'm a little scared. Can you **come over**?
Her friends **came over** yesterday and stayed all afternoon.

Come on over is an informal invitation that emphasizes that the distance is really short.

I hear a lot of noise coming **Come on over** and join the party!
   from your house!

To **go ahead** means to continue with one's plans.

I'm ready to leave.	Then **go ahead!**
We're going to see that horror movie.	**Go ahead.** But don't say I didn't warn you.

To **go ahead and** + **basic verb** means to encourage someone to do something he or she may be hesitating about.

I'm not sure about this car.	**Go ahead and** buy it. It's a good deal.

To **go ahead and** do something is also a way of saying that you are going to do it right away.

Will you send me more information about your products?	OK, I'll **go ahead and** e-mail you our brochure.
I'm going to **go ahead and** make the reservation for seven o'clock.	

Ace

To **ace** means to get a very good grade with little effort.

> I didn't know he was so smart. He's **acing** trigonometry.

Fancy

Fancy is used to describe something elegant, possibly with intricate details.

> She wore a very **fancy** dress with lots of ruffles and bows.
> It was a **fancy** party. There were flowers and candles everywhere, and there was a seven-course, sit-down dinner for more than a hundred guests.

Any chance . . . ?

Any chance . . . ? is used to ask informally if something is possible or true.

> **Any chance** you have a lawn mower I could borrow?
> **Any chance** we could get together for a cup of coffee?

How about if . . . ?

The expression **how about if . . . ?** offers a suggestion for action by one or more people.

> We have a long weekend coming up. **How about if** we all go to the beach?
> I know you don't have enough money to buy the car. **How about if** I lend it to you?

I'll get back to you

I'll get back to you is a promise to find information for someone and contact him or her as soon as you have it.

> I don't know how much the real estate tax on this house is, but I'll find out and **get back to you** right away.

ASAP

ASAP means as soon as possible.

> Call me **ASAP.** I have to make up my mind tonight, and I need your advice.

Instead

Instead indicates a replacement for something else. It is placed *after* the word that indicates the replacement.

> We thought about going to the beach, but went to the mountains **instead**.

Instead of is used *before* the replaced alternative.

> He bought a truck **instead of** a car.
> We went to the mountains **instead of** going to the beach.
> **Instead of** going to the beach, we went to the mountains.

By the way

By the way introduces a new topic or a change in subject in the middle of a conversation.

> Yes, I really like my new job. **By the way**, have you heard from Kevin?
> Sophia said she would take care of the dog while we're away. **By the way**, are you still willing to water the plants?

Don't hesitate

Don't hesitate is a way to indicate your willingness to be available for someone.

> If you have any questions about this contract, **don't hesitate** to call me.

See you later

See you later is an informal way of saying good-bye. Alternative expressions include **see ya/later/bye/ciao**.

> OK, I've gotta run. **See you later.**

EXERCISE
7·1

Circle the most appropriate expression for each situation.

1. You are ready to order a meal in a restaurant. You say to the server:
   a. I want the chicken.
   b. I'd like the chicken, please.
   c. Can you bring me the chicken?
   d. Would you bring me the chicken?

2. A woman has just fallen down and cannot get up. You say to someone with a phone:
   a. Would you mind calling an ambulance?
   b. Could you call an ambulance?
   c. Would you like to call an ambulance, please?
   d. Call an ambulance!

3. Your car has broken down and your cell phone's battery is dead. You say to a stranger:
   a. Would you mind if I borrowed your cell phone to call my mechanic?
   b. Hey, can I borrow your phone?
   c. Let me use your phone!
   d. Give me your phone, please.

4. You are talking with your academic adviser at the university. You say:
   a. How many credits should I get in order to graduate?
   b. How many credits may I get in order to graduate?
   c. How many credits could I get in order to graduate?
   d. How many credits do I need to get in order to graduate?

5. A tow truck has come to take your car to the mechanic's garage. You say to the driver:
   a. Would you like to give me a ride to the garage?
   b. Give me a ride to the garage!
   c. Can you give me a ride to the garage?
   d. I'm willing to ride with you to the garage.

6. A poll is being taken concerning an upcoming election. You say:
   a. I need Walters to win.
   b. I have to have Walters win.
   c. I would want Walters to win.
   d. I want Walters to win.

Write an appropriate question or command for each situation.

1. You want the lady in front of you in the theater to take off her large hat so you can see.

   _____

2. You want to borrow a ladder from your neighbor.

   _____

3. You want a friend to lend you $20.

   _____

4. You want your brother to lend you $20.

   _____

5. You are in Washington, D.C. You want a stranger on the street to give you directions to the White House.

   _____

6. You want to borrow a pen from your classmate.

   _____

7. You want the fire department to come to your house to put out a fire.

   _____

8. You want a taxi driver to take you to the airport.

   _____

9. You are in a car with several friends. You want the driver to drop you off at the next corner.

_____

10. A friend is giving you a ride home. You want him to turn right at the next stoplight.

_____

EXERCISE

7·3

Write an appropriate question or statement offering assistance for each of the following situations.

1. An eight-year-old boy has just fallen off his bicycle and scraped his knee.

_____

2. You are at a party with your small child who will not stop crying and wants to go home.

_____

3. Your best friend is having a party for one hundred people at her home.

_____

4. Your brother didn't get a paycheck last month.

_____

5. One of your coworkers seems to be having a heart attack.

_____

6. Your neighbor is going on vacation for two weeks.

_____

7. You are a sales assistant at a shoe store. A customer is looking at several pairs of shoes.

_____

8. You are a customer service representative at a large company. A woman has just approached your desk.

_____

9. You and your wife discover that your car has been stolen.

_____

10. A couple of tourists look lost.

_____

EXERCISE
7·4

Match the words and expressions in the first column with those in the second column that have a similar meaning. Note: There may be more than one match for each expression.

1. _____ be willing
2. _____ ace
3. _____ mind
4. _____ be back on track
5. _____ come over
6. _____ go over
7. _____ miss
8. _____ be on top of it

a. answer incorrectly on a test
b. be bothered
c. be happy to
d. be sad thinking about
e. get a good grade on a test
f. get over a difficult period
g. have under control
h. lose an opportunity
i. not arrive on time for public transportation
j. not attend an event
k. not be happy about
l. not mind doing
m. recover from lost time
n. review
o. visit a neighbor

EXERCISE
7·5

Circle the most appropriate response to each question or remark.

1. Hurry up! I don't want to miss the train.
   a. We'll be back on track.
   b. You'll miss me.
   c. We'll go ahead and walk.
   d. Go ahead without me.

2. Good news! The judge dismissed the lawsuit against you.
   a. Don't hesitate to call me.
   b. That's a load off my mind.
   c. I'm on top of it.
   d. I'm back on track.

3. You missed ten out of twenty questions on the exam.
   a. Any chance you can help me?
   b. Do you mind?
   c. That's a load off my mind.
   d. I aced it.

4. Are you willing to work harder?
   a. I'll work instead.
   b. By the way, don't hesitate.
   c. I'll get back on track.
   d. I'm not on top of it.

5. Do you mind if I call you?
   a. That's a load off my shoulders.
   b. Go over there.
   c. Of course not. Don't hesitate.
   d. Oh yeah?

EXERCISE
7·6

Write an answer for each of the following questions. Ask an English-speaking friend to check your answers.

1. What do you do if you miss a bus, train, or airplane?

   _____

2. Do you miss a person or place? What does it feel like?

   _____

3. What do you do if you miss a question on a test?

   _____

4. What do you do if you miss a class or a day of work?

   _____

5. In what games can you miss the ball?

   _____

EXERCISE
7·7

Write a question or remark for each of the following answers. Ask an English-speaking friend to check your work.

1. _____

   Go ahead. I don't mind.

2. _____

   Don't hesitate to call me.

3. _____

   That's totally awesome.

4. _____

That's a load off my shoulders.

5. _____

What can I do to help you?

6. _____

I'll call the doctor.

7. _____

I'll come over right away.

8. _____

Sure, I'll go over it with you.

9. _____

Don't miss this opportunity!

10. _____

The thing is, I've been really busy.

Write a conversation between two people in which both ask for and offer favors to each other. Use at least eight of the expressions explained in this chapter. Ask an English-speaking friend to check your work.

_____

_____

_____

_____

_____

_____

_____

_____

_____

_____

Expressing doubts and uncertainty

Conversation: Advice to a friend

PAT: Hi, Katie—I'm calling you to **cry on your shoulder**. **Do you mind** if I come over? I really need to talk to you.

KATIE: Of course I don't mind; come over. I'll make a pot of tea. Pat, what's **the matter**?

PAT: It's just that everything is wrong with my life. **In the first place**, there are **so** many problems at work. My boss is really **out to get** me. He's **on my case** for every little thing. Lately I can't do anything that pleases him. **Plus**, he makes me **so** nervous that I'm beginning to make unnecessary mistakes.

KATIE: **So**, what's the reason for all that?

PAT: It's probably because he has problems at home. But that doesn't give him the right to **take it all out on** me, does it?

KATIE: It's **just the opposite**. It's at work where he ought to seek a little peace **so** he can **work out** his personal problems at home. **At least** that's what I think.

PAT: I have the impression that nobody is really happy. The situation at my house **doesn't exactly** cheer me up either. You know what? Those two guys I share the house with **don't have a clue** about how to keep it clean. They **don't lift a finger** to help me. Last night I **spent** two hours cleaning the kitchen while they **pigged out** on pizza and watched TV. I'm **sick and tired** of their behavior. But that's not the worst! **As if that weren't enough**, Brad refuses to talk to me. Like **out of the blue** he's decided he **wants his space**. I really feel like **throwing in the towel**.

KATIE: Calm down, Pat, and **let's** look at one thing at a time. I don't think things are as bad as they seem right now. **For a start**, **why don't** we make a list of the positive things in your life? That way, you'll realize what your **strengths** are. Then we'll make a plan to begin changing the things that aren't **working** for you. You shouldn't let yourself get depressed.

PAT: Thanks, Katie. You know, I already feel much better. You really know how to **cheer me up**.

KATIE: I care about you. **After all**, you are my best friend—and have been **from the get-go**. I know I can **count on** you for good advice **from time to time**.

Improving your conversation

In the first place

In the first place is an expression that precedes the first point or argument you present when trying to convince someone of something.

> I don't want to live in the southern part of the county. **In the first place**, the schools are not very good there.

For a start

For a start is an expression that precedes the first suggestion related to a plan.

> We both want to buy a new house, but **for a start**, we need to see if we have enough money.

Alternatives to this expression are **for starters** and **to begin with**.

> I will consider your marriage proposal, but **for starters**, we need to work out some of our problems.
> Let's talk about our plans for the new house. **To begin with**, we need to decide exactly what we want.

Plus

Plus introduces a second, third, or further point in a positive or negative argument.

> I loved that movie. It was a western; Clint Eastwood was in it; **plus**, it lasted three hours.
> I hated that movie. It was a western; Clint Eastwood was in it; **plus**, it lasted three hours.

In addition

In addition introduces a second, third, or further point in a positive argument. In the following example, it is understood that the speaker likes westerns, likes Clint Eastwood, and was happy that the movie was long.

> I loved that movie. It was a western; Clint Eastwood was in it; **in addition**, it lasted three hours.

Besides

Besides introduces a second, third, or further point in a negative or defensive argument. In the following example, it is understood that the speaker does not like westerns, does not like Clint Eastwood, and was unhappy that the movie was long.

> I hated that movie. It was a western; Clint Eastwood was in it; **besides**, it lasted three hours.

As if that weren't enough

As if that weren't enough introduces a final point at the end of a series of positive or negative arguments.

> It was a terrible date. He arrived late. He was rude to my parents. And **as if that weren't enough**, he was in a bad mood the whole evening.

At least

At least indicates a minimum possible amount.

> You have **at least** $100 in your pocket (possibly more).
> He has **at least** three cars!

At least can introduce a comment intended to show that something is good, in spite of other negative information.

> It's cold and rainy, but **at least** I have my umbrella.

After all

After all introduces a reason or a justification of what was just said.

> Don't expect him to behave like an adult. **After all**, he's only ten years old.
> I didn't do my best at work today, but **after all**, I was sick.

Cry on someone's shoulder

To **cry on someone's shoulder** means to tell someone that you need sympathy and support.

> I just got fired from my job. Will you let me **cry on your shoulder** tonight?

Matter

To **matter** means to be important.

> You really **matter** to me a lot.
> I'm sorry I hurt your feelings.　　　　It doesn't **matter**. (It's not important.) I forgive you.

To be **the matter** indicates what is wrong or what is upsetting someone.

> You've been crying. What's **the matter**?
> I just heard that my brother is sick.　　　　Do you know what's **the matter** with him?

Just the opposite

To be **just the opposite** indicates that the truth is very different from what was just said.

> You must be really excited about your promotion!　　　　It's **just the opposite**! They're transferring me to another city, and I don't want to go.

Out to get

To be **out to get** someone means to want to hurt or make trouble for that person.

> The president of the club refused to listen to any of our suggestions. I think he is really **out to get** us.

On someone's case

To be **on someone's case** means to constantly criticize or scold someone.

> My dad's always **on my case** about my long hair. He really wants me to cut it.

Take it all out on

To **take it all out on** someone means to build up anger and frustration over a problem and then show that anger toward a person unrelated to the problem.

> I know you're disappointed that you didn't get better grades at school, but don't **take it out on** your little sister!

Work out

To **work out** a problem is to solve it.

> We're not going to get married until we can **work out** our problems.

To **work out** can also mean to be satisfactory.

> The new arrangement of desks at the office is **working out** very well. Everybody likes it.
> Our relationship isn't **working out**. It's better that we not see each other anymore.

To **work out** can also mean to exercise.

> You look fantastic—I can tell you've been **working out**.

Not have a clue

To **not have a clue** means to not know what is happening or what others are thinking.

> Do you think Ray has any acting talent?   To be honest with you, I do**n't** think he **has a clue** about what he's supposed to be doing.

Not lift a finger

To **not lift a finger** means to not do anything to help or contribute.

> She is so spoiled. She does**n't lift a finger** to help her parents with the housework.

Spend

To **spend** means to use money or time.

> Oh my gosh! I just **spent** $100 on groceries.
> I wish you wouldn't **spend** so much time playing video games.

Pig out

To **pig out** means to eat too much.

> Oh, I really **pigged out** on that cake. It was so delicious.

Sick and tired

To be **sick and tired** means to no longer tolerate something.

> He's been here pigging out all week. I'm **sick and tired** of his behavior.

Out of the blue

To be **out of the blue** means to appear or happen with no warning.

> So I'm driving down the turnpike when **out of the blue** I get a call from Freddie!

Want one's space

To **want one's space** is a delicate way of saying you want to end a romantic relationship.

> Elizabeth, we've been arguing a lot lately, and I'm getting uncomfortable with it. I really feel like I **want my space** for a while, so I can think things over.

Throw in the towel

To **throw in the towel** means to stop trying to do something. An alternative expression is to **give up**.

Hey, Niko, how are your tennis lessons going?

Oh, I **threw in the towel** a couple of months ago. I just didn't have enough time to practice.

I have to quit school; it's just too hard.

You can't **give up** now! You only have a couple of semesters left.

Work

To be **working for** someone can mean to be employed by that person.

I'm still going to school, but I'm **working for** my dad this summer.

It can also indicate that a certain strategy or program is suitable for someone.

This new diet just isn't **working for** me. I've actually gained weight!
Teaching at the public school really **works for** her, because she has the same schedule as her children.

Cheer someone up

To **cheer someone up** means to make someone feel happier.

She was feeling lonely, so we went over and **cheered her up**.

Count on

To **count on** someone means to expect that that person will support you when necessary. Alternative expressions are to **depend on** someone and to **rely on** someone.

We can always **count on** Bob to make us laugh.
She doesn't worry about spending money; she knows she can **depend on** her mother to pay her bills.
You're always late! I can't **rely on** you when I need you.

To **be there for** someone means to support someone whenever necessary.

I **count on** Ann. She **is** always **there for** me.
He's a great dad, always **there for** his kids.

Do you mind . . . ?

Do you mind . . . ? is a way of asking someone's permission to do something.

Do you mind if I sit here?
Do you mind if I smoke?

No, of course not. (You may sit there.)
Actually, I do. Smoke really bothers me.

Let's

Let's is a way of suggesting an activity for you and one or more other people.

Let's eat Chinese tonight.
Let's not argue about it.

Why don't . . . ?

Why don't . . . ? is another way of suggesting an activity to one or more people. This may or may not include you.

> **Why don't** you study Japanese?
> **Why don't** we invite the neighbors over?

Strengths

Strengths are the positive traits of a person. The negative traits are called **weaknesses**.

> Often in a job interview, they ask you what your **strengths** and **weaknesses** are. It's a good idea to emphasize your **strengths**.

So

So has a number of uses. **So many** emphasizes that there are a lot.

> She has **so many** friends on Facebook, she can't keep in touch with them all.

So + adjective means very.

> He is **so** funny—he makes everybody laugh.

So can indicate—or ask for—a conclusion as a response to new information.

> We don't have enough money to buy a new
>   house, **so** we have to get extra jobs.
> I don't want to buy a new dress.   **So** what are you going to wear to the wedding?

Not exactly

Not exactly, when used before an adjective or a noun, means not at all.

> She's **not exactly** shy. (She's aggressive.)
> He's **not exactly** a stranger. (We know him well.)

Hardly can be used with the same meaning.

> He's **hardly** my best friend. (We are rivals.)
> It's **hardly** rocket science. (It's not difficult.)

From the get-go

From the get-go means from the beginning.

> He has been enthusiastic about this project **from the get-go**.
> She's been a pain in the neck **from the get-go**. Let's get her off the committee.

From time to time

From time to time means sometimes. Other expressions with the same meaning are **(every) once in a while/(every) now and then/every so often/occasionally**. These expressions can go before the subject or at the end of the phrase.

> I'm not still in love with him, but I think of him **from time to time**.
> She's not a big football fan, but **every once in a while** she goes to a game with me.

Now and then he sends me an e-mail.
We have a family reunion **every so often**.
Occasionally I get together with my high school friends.

8·1

Fill in each blank with the most appropriate word or expression (after all, besides, in the first place, in addition, plus, as if that weren't enough, at least).

1. I like the house on Oak Street. a. _____, it's in a good neighborhood.
b. _____, it's in a great school district, c. _____, it's close enough to the school for the kids to walk. d. _____, the price is under our budget, and we'd have money for decorating. You're right, it's not really close to a shopping center, but e. _____, that's not the most important thing to us. f. _____ we have a reliable car for trips to the grocery store.

2. I hope you don't choose a college on the other side of the country. a. _____, we can't afford out-of-state tuition. b. _____, the in-state tuition is much lower. c. _____, our state universities are among the best in the country. d. _____, think how expensive it would be for you to come home for holidays.

8·2

Fill in each blank with in addition *or* besides, *as appropriate.*

1. I don't want to go to school today. It's really boring, and _____, I have a bad headache.

2. I didn't enjoy the game. There wasn't much action, and _____, we lost.

3. The birthday party was awesome! There was a clown who did really cool tricks, and _____, there was a huge chocolate cake.

4. I really want to move to New York. It has interesting neighborhoods, great restaurants, and fantastic museums. _____, you can get around easily on public transportation.

5. No, we can't move to New York. It's too far away from my family, it's expensive, and _____, you don't even have a job there!

Match the words or expressions in the first column with those in the second column that have a similar meaning. Note: There may be more than one match for each expression.

1. _____ cry on someone's shoulder
2. _____ take it out on someone
3. _____ be the matter
4. _____ matter
5. _____ be out to get someone
6. _____ be on someone's case
7. _____ be sick and tired of
8. _____ count on someone
9. _____ be working for someone
10. _____ be there for someone
11. _____ cheer someone up
12. _____ want one's space

a. be someone's employee
b. be suitable for someone
c. be weary of
d. be wrong
e. blame an innocent person
f. criticize someone
g. give unconditional support to someone
h. intend to hurt someone
i. want to end a relationship with someone
j. no longer tolerate
k. be important
l. not want to do anymore
m. depend on someone
n. not want to hear anymore
o. scold someone
p. tell someone your problems
q. make someone feel better
r. know someone will be there for you

Circle the most appropriate response to each question or remark.

1. I can't handle this anymore.
   a. Don't lift a finger.
   b. Get off my case.
   c. You can cry on my shoulder.
   d. I'm sick and tired.

2. She criticizes everything I do.
   a. Why is she there for you?
   b. Why is she on your case?
   c. Why does she cheer you up?
   d. Why does she cry on your shoulder?

3. He asked me for a date.
   a. I think he's out to get you.
   b. I think he wants his space.
   c. I think he likes you.
   d. I think he's on your case.

4. Why are you so upset?
   a. My boyfriend wants his space.
   b. My boyfriend just pigged out.
   c. My boyfriend is there for me.
   d. My boyfriend works out.

5. What are his strengths?
   a. He doesn't lift a finger.
   b. I don't have a clue.
   c. He's out to get me.
   d. He spends too much time on the telephone.

EXERCISE
8·5

Circle the word or expression that best completes each of the following sentences.

1. I really _____ tonight. Now I don't feel so good.
   a. worked out
   b. pigged out
   c. mattered
   d. cheered her up

2. He's my best friend. He's always _____.
   a. wanting his space
   b. working for someone
   c. there for me
   d. pigging out

3. They _____ a lot of time fixing this place up.
   a. worked out
   b. counted on
   c. spent
   d. wanted their space

4. Thank you! That really _____.
   a. cheers me up
   b. lifts a finger
   c. spends a lot of money
   d. is on my case

5. He spends a lot of money, so he must be rich. It's _____; he hardly has enough to pay his rent.
   a. out of the blue
   b. just the opposite
   c. a strength
   d. the matter

EXERCISE
8·6

Circle the most appropriate response to each question or remark.

1. Is it true you have a great new office manager?
   a. Yes, she doesn't lift a finger.
   b. Yes, she is on your case.
   c. Yes, she doesn't have a clue.
   d. Yes, she is working out.

2. You look fantastic!
   a. Thanks, I've been pigging out.
   b. Thanks, I've been working out.
   c. Thanks, I've been lifting a finger.
   d. Thanks, I've been wanting my space.

Expressing doubts and uncertainty   89

3. Can I count on you?
   a. Of course, I am sick and tired.
   b. Of course, I don't have a clue.
   c. Of course, I am always there for you.
   d. Of course, I am on your case.

4. Do you mind if I sit here?
   a. Of course not, go right ahead.
   b. Of course, go right ahead.
   c. Of course not, you may not sit there.
   d. Of course, I'm sick and tired.

5. Can I cry on your shoulder?
   a. Of course. I'm on your case.
   b. Of course. What's the matter?
   c. Of course. I'll take it out on you.
   d. Of course. I'm out to get you.

EXERCISE
8·7

Write a question or remark for each of the following responses. Ask an English-speaking friend to check your work.

1. _____

   Yes, it works for me.

2. _____

   She doesn't lift a finger.

3. _____

   Yes, he's really on my case.

4. _____

   Yes, they're always there for me.

5. _____

   No, I don't mind.

EXERCISE
8·8

Match the words or expressions in the first column with those in the second column that have a similar meaning. Note: There may be more than one match for each expression.

1. _____ hardly

2. _____ so

3. _____ the get-go

4. _____ so many

5. _____ plus

a. a lot of

b. besides

c. every now and then

d. every so often

e. for a start

6. _____ after all
7. _____ from time to time
8. _____ to begin with

f. in addition
g. it's logical that
h. not exactly
i. occasionally
j. the beginning
k. then
l. very

Answer the following questions in complete sentences. Ask an English-speaking friend to check your answers.

1. Who is always there for you?

_____

2. What happened recently in your life out of the blue?

_____

3. What do you spend a lot of time doing?

_____

4. Who counts on you? What do you do for that person?

_____

5. What cheers you up? Why?

_____

Write a paragraph in which you try to convince someone to agree with your opinion or viewpoint on a topic that matters to you. Use at least eight of the expressions explained in this chapter. Ask an English-speaking friend to check your work.

_____

_____

_____

_____

_____

_____

_____

_____

_____

_____

_____

Talking about future events

Conversation A: Scheduled events

RAJ: What time does the movie **start**?

INES: It **starts** at 7:30, and **ends** at 9:45.

RAJ: Good, we can go on the bus, and get back home before it's too dark. Is there a bus stop near your house?

INES: Yes. It **stops** on the corner every fifteen minutes.

RAJ: Perfect. I'm looking forward to seeing this movie.

Conversation B: Plans for the very near future

JENNY: What are you **doing** tomorrow?

PAULA: I'm going to the beach with my family for a week. We're leaving early—at 6 a.m.

JENNY: Oh, nice! So I guess you're **planning** to go to bed early tonight.

PAULA: Yeah, I'm **gonna** pack my bag and try to **hit the sack** by nine o'clock.

JENNY: **Good luck with that!** What are you taking?

PAULA: I always **pack light** for the beach—a bathing suit, a couple of pairs of shorts, some T-shirts, a hat, and lots of sunscreen. How about you? What are you doing next week?

JENNY: I'm **going to** stay home and **catch up on** some unfinished projects.

PAULA: Like what?

JENNY: Oh, I have a long list! First I'm **going to** clean up my office, pay bills, write letters, and **take care of a bunch of** paperwork. Then I'm **going to** redecorate my bedroom—paint the walls and get new curtains.

PAULA: Wow. What color are you **going to** paint it?

JENNY: It's a very light blue. I've already picked it out and bought the paint.

PAULA: Cool.

Conversation C: Long-term plans

EMMA: What do you think **you'll** do when you finish college?

KIM: Oh, **I'll probably** stay in the city and look for work here. Then I'll go back home on holidays.

EMMA: I love that idea, but **I'll probably** go closer to home to get a job. I like being close to my family and old friends. **Still**, life in the big city is certainly tempting!

KIM: Well, **maybe** you could find a job in a big city closer to home.

EMMA: Yeah, that would be a good **happy medium**.

KIM: **On the other hand**, **since** you like to travel, you could possibly get a job in another country—do something exotic.

EMMA: You're right. I **might** get really bored just doing **the same old thing**. I'd learn a lot **overseas**—even **pick up** another language. It's definitely something to think about.

KIM: Well, I guess we don't have to decide now, since we're still in our **freshman** year!

Conversation D: Predictions for the more distant future

TEACHER: What will the world be like fifty years from now?

ANDY: **Just think!** People **will** be living on Mars.

EMILY: **I'll bet** cars **will** be replaced by little helicopters, so you'll be able to fly ahead in traffic.

HOLLY: There **won't** be any more wars.

JULIE: Women **will** make more money than men.

STACEY: **No way!** Women **will** stay home and the men **will** do all the work.

JOE: There **will** be a better form of government.

ZACK: People **will** have forgotten how to talk and **will** only communicate electronically.

HEATHER: There **won't** be any disease, and people **will** live to be 150 years old.

COURTNEY: That **will** be horrible. It **will** be so crowded!

ANDY: That's why people **will** be living on Mars!

Improving your conversation

No one can say for sure what will happen in the future, yet we often talk about it. Future events can be described in several different ways, depending on how probable it is that they will happen.

Scheduled events

The present tense is used to talk about the future. It is used to give the time of scheduled events (99 percent probability).

> The flight **leaves** at four o'clock this afternoon.
> The movie **starts** at five o'clock, so don't be late.

The present tense is also used to tell what normally happens and is expected to be the same in the future (99 percent probability).

> The stores **open** at ten o'clock tomorrow morning.
> The children **go** back to school in September.
> Class **ends** at 3:15.
> The train **stops** near our building every hour.

I'll bet

The present tense is used after the expression **I'll bet**, meaning I'm pretty sure it will happen.

> **I'll bet** she wins the election.
> **I'll bet** he calls me as soon as he gets home.

Going to

To be **going to** is used to indicate events planned for the near future (95 percent probability).

> We're **going to** move to our new house next month.
> They're **going to** get married in June.

In informal conversation, **going to** is often pronounced "**gonna**."

> I'm **gonna** go see my grandmother this afternoon.

The present progressive (**basic verb + -ing**) can be used as an alternative to **going to** (95 percent probability).

> We're **moving** to our new house next month.
> They're **getting** married in June.
> We're **planning** to go to the game tomorrow.
> I'll be **doing** homework after school.

Will probably

Will probably + **basic verb** is used to indicate about a 75 percent probability of happening.

> She**'ll probably** be late.
> We**'ll probably** leave early.

Probably won't + **basic verb** is used to indicate about a 25 percent probability of happening.

> He **probably won't** come with me.
> You **probably won't** like this movie.

May/might

May or **might** + **basic verb** can be used to express about a 50 percent possibility of something happening.

> He **may** be late, because he has to work until 6.
> She **might** be late, too.
> I **might** come over tomorrow. It depends on what time I get home.

Maybe

Maybe also expresses about a 50 percent possibility of something happening. Unlike **may** and **might**, it is placed before the subject.

> **Maybe** they'll be late.
> **Maybe** I'll come over tomorrow.

Will

Will + basic verb is tricky, as it can indicate both very high and very low probability. It is used to make a promise (99 percent probability).

> I**'ll** be here at six tomorrow morning.
> We**'ll** call you as soon as we arrive.

It is also used to predict the more distant future (10 percent probability).

> My baby **will** be a doctor when he grows up.
> You **will** get married and have a bunch of children.

Won't

Won't + basic verb indicates a very low probability that something will happen.

> He **won't** be at the wedding.
> We **won't** be able to see you in such a big crowd.

Hit the sack

Hit the sack is a very informal way to say to go to bed and sleep.

> Man, I was exhausted last night. I **hit the sack** as soon as I got home.

Pack light

To **pack light** means to prepare only a very small suitcase or carry-on for traveling.

> Be sure to **pack light**, because we'll have to carry our bags part of the way.

Catch up on

To **catch up on** means to do or learn something that you didn't do earlier.

> When we're at the beach, I plan to **catch up on** some important reading.

Take care of

To **take care of** can mean to perform a task.

> I was going to call a plumber, but my husband said he would **take care of** it.
> Will you mow the lawn for me?   Sure, I'll **take care of** it.

Take care of can also mean to attend to a child or other person needing supervision.

> They're looking for someone to **take care of** her ninety-year-old mother during the day.

Pick up

To **pick up** means to grasp something that is on a lower surface.

> I broke the glass and had to **pick up** all the pieces.

It can also mean to lift.

> This box is too heavy. We can't **pick** it **up**.

Pick up can also mean to meet and give a ride to someone.

> You can go with us. We'll be glad to **pick** you **up**.

To **pick up** can also mean to learn easily.

> I don't think you can **pick up** Italian just by going to Venice on a vacation.
> Of course, you will **pick up** a few useful phrases.

Happy medium

To reach a **happy medium** means to agree by accepting some parts of one argument and some parts of the opposing argument.

> His style was modern, and hers was traditional. They reached a **happy medium** by buying an old house and putting in modern furniture.

A verb with the same meaning is to **compromise**.

> The only way to keep everybody happy is to **compromise**.

A bunch of

A (whole) **bunch of** means a lot of. Alternative expressions include **quite a few** and **a number of**.

> **A whole bunch of** friends are coming over tonight.
> She has **quite a few** admirers.
> There are still **a number of** tickets available.

The same old thing

The **same old thing** is a way to indicate that activities are routine.

> What are you up to these days?   Oh, you know, the **same old thing**—working, taking care of the kids, going to school at night.

On the other hand

On the other hand is an expression that introduces an argument that is contrary to—or opposite to—a previously mentioned argument.

> Well, we could use our savings to buy the house. **On the other hand**, we could use the money to visit your family in Ethiopia.

Since

Since can mean because, usually indicating that something is convenient.

> I don't have an appointment for a haircut, but **since** I was in the neighborhood, I stopped by to see if you had time for me.
> I was going to go home early today, but **since** you're here, I'll do your hair.

Since can also indicate the beginning of a time period.

> She's been studying English **since** last September.
> I've been waiting for you **since** four o'clock.

Still

Still has several meanings. In the example conversations, it introduces information that the speaker feels is contrary to the previous information, indicating a dilemma.

> I'd love to buy the house. **Still**, it's important to go visit my family.

Overseas/abroad

Overseas refers to places on the other side of the ocean. **Abroad** refers to all countries except the one you are in.

> We lived **overseas** for a number of years.
> Many college students have the opportunity to study **abroad**.

Freshman

Freshman refers to a student in the first year of high school or college. It can also be another name for the first year. Second-year students are called **sophomores**; third-year students are **juniors**, and fourth-year students are **seniors**.

> She may look like a **freshman**, but actually she's in her **senior** year.
> This is the biggest **freshman** class we've ever had.

Senior (citizen) can also refer to a person who is sixty years old or more.

> He's a **senior** in high school, and his grandmother is a **senior**.

Just think

Just think is an expression that introduces a fantasy or real plan the speaker is excited about.

> **Just think!** We could get married and have children.
> **Just think!** This time tomorrow we'll be in Rome!

Good luck with that

Good luck with that is an expression indicating that the speaker doesn't think the previous statement is very likely to happen.

They told me I'd win $500 if I wrote the best essay.	**Good luck with that.** They told the same thing to all the elementary school students in the whole city.

No way

No way indicates that something is impossible, unbelievable—or even wonderful.

Are you going to major in chemistry?	**No way!** There's **no way** I'm going to spend four years working in a laboratory.
John and Mary are getting married next month.	**No way!** They were fighting the last time I saw them.
I'm going to Denmark for two weeks.	**No way!** Lucky you!

Fill in each blank with the most appropriate word or words.

1. When you grow up, you _____ rich and famous.
   a. are being   c. will be
   b. are   d. were

2. Can you join us tomorrow? That's impossible because we _____ sightseeing.
   a. went   c. will go
   b. are going   d. go

3. Don't be late. The show _____ at 6:30.
   a. will start   c. started
   b. is starting   d. starts

4. Will you go to the party with me on Friday night? I can't. I _____.
   a. study this weekend   c. am going to stay in
   b. will stay in   d. might

5. I'm not sure what to do. _____
   a. Maybe I'll take the job.   c. I won't take the job.
   b. I'll take the job.   d. I'm taking the job.

6. Is your brother going to the circus with you? _____
   a. No. He doesn't go.   c. No. He won't go.
   b. No. Maybe he doesn't go.   d. No. He is going.

Match the words and expressions in the first column with those in the second column that have a similar meaning. Note: There may be more than one match for each expression.

1. _____ go to bed   a. attend to someone

2. _____ pack light   b. compromise

3. _____ catch up on   c. do

4. _____ take care of   d. do something you didn't do earlier

5. _____ pick up   e. give a ride to

6. _____ reach a happy medium   f. hit the sack

                                      g. learn a little

                                      h. learn something you missed

                                      i. lift

                                      j. take a small suitcase

Circle the word or expression that best completes each of the following sentences.

1. Our mayor is an excellent politician. _____, he's not exactly a good administrator.
   a. Just think   b. No way   c. On the other hand

2. I'll probably take his course. _____, I've heard he's a hard grader.
   a. Still   b. Just think   c. No way

3. It's great to have a holiday. _____, otherwise we'd be at the office right now.
   a. Just think   b. No way   c. Still

4. I'm exhausted. I'll probably _____ as soon as I get home.
   a. hit the sack   b. pack light   c. reach a happy medium

5. I'm going to ask the teacher to give me an A in this course. _____!
   a. Still   b. Just think   c. Good luck with that

Fill in each blank with an appropriate word or expression that is explained in this chapter.

1. There aren't very many jobs available. _____, I'm going to keep looking.

2. He's seventy-five, so he gets a _____ discount.

3. We're so bored. It seems like every day we do _____.

4. Maybe if I got a job _____, I could pick up another language.

5. There will be _____ new students next year.

6. I heard the _____ class is going to be the biggest one ever.

7. You have a lot of airport changes on this trip. You really should _____.

8. She's staying at home tonight to _____ some reading.

9. I tried to pay for the dinner, but he insisted on _____ it.

10. He wants an apartment, and she wants a house. They could _____ by buying a townhouse.

Write a question or remark for each of the following responses. Ask an English-speaking friend to check your work.

1. _____

   I'll take care of it!

2. _____

   I'll take care of her!

3. _____

   Still, I'm not sure it's a good idea.

4. _____

   We could pick up a little Arabic.

5. _____

   On the other hand, it's very expensive.

6. _____

   Just think! We'll be having so much fun!

7. _____

   She won't go.

8. _____

   Good luck with that!

9. _____

   No way!

10. _____

   That sounds like a good happy medium.

Write a letter to a friend in which you tell of your plans for today and tomorrow and of your hopes and dreams for the future. Use all of the future expressions explained in this chapter. Ask an English-speaking friend to check your work.

_____

_____

_____

_____

_____

_____

_____

_____

_____

_____

Making a case or arguing a point

Conversation: Selecting a company officer

Boss: I've called you here to talk about the selection of a new director for the Customer Service Department. As you know, **so far** there are only two candidates, Martha Francis and Juliette Welch. **First**, I'd like to hear your comments, both **pro** and **con**, about Martha's qualifications for this position.

Ivana: Well, I think Martha is the perfect person for this position. She's been with the company for twenty years, so she knows the business **inside out**. She's conservative and serious; **plus** she gets along with everybody.

April: **Yikes!** In my opinion, if she becomes director, nothing will change. **I mean**, we wouldn't see anything new—just the opposite—we'd **keep on** implementing the same programs as always.

Katie: She isn't known for **thinking outside the box**. **What's more**, we'd start to see our current customer base **fall off**, simply because our competitors have enthusiastic new people and innovative programs. I'm **just sayin'** . . .

Tim: I have to agree with April and Katie on this one. **In the first place**, Martha is too conservative; **plus** she'd **hardly** inspire any enthusiasm among the employees.

Boss: Anybody else want to **put their two cents in**? OK. Then let's talk about Juliette. What do **you guys** think?

Ivana: Look, if Juliette gets this job, it will be a **total** disaster for the company. **In the first place**, her fancy degree isn't worth **squat** because she has **zero** experience. **Besides**, we don't even know her very well. **Good grief**, she's only been here **since** March, and **to top it all off**, we all know that she was fired from her last job.

Tim: **Really**. I've heard that her coworkers think she's **a bit uppity**, like she thinks she's the queen of the office. She's **not exactly** popular with the other employees. I don't think they'd be happy with her as the boss.

Stan: Well, **since** I **put her name up**, I have to say that I see her as a very bright and competent person. **Still**, I recognize that she lacks experience. And now that you tell me that her personality could cause **friction** among the employees, then I'll **go along with** your decision in this case.

Boss: **Obviously**, we haven't found the ideal person to **handle** this job. We may have to look outside the company, which I don't particularly want to do. We'll meet here tomorrow at the same time. I'll expect your suggestions—and **they'd better** be more promising!

Improving your conversation

Pros and cons

Pro can be used as a shortened form of *professional*—in this case meaning expert.

> You painted the walls yourself? Man, you're a real **pro**!

Pro can refer to the positive characteristics or positions in an argument. **Con** refers to the negative ones.

> This issue has both **pros** and **cons**.
> On the **pro** side, he's a hard worker.
> On the **con** side, he often comes to work late.

In the first place/plus/in addition

To begin a series of arguments that are intended to convince someone to agree with your **pro** (positive) argument, use **in the first place**. Subsequent arguments are introduced by **in the second place**, **in addition** (more formal), **furthermore** (more formal), **what's more**, **plus**, and—to introduce the last argument—**finally**. **For the frosting on the cake** can be used instead of **finally** to indicate that the last argument mentioned is the strongest one of all. **As if that weren't enough** and **to top it all off** are alternative expressions with the same function.

> Our lake district is a wonderful place for a vacation. **In the first place**, it's easily reached by car, and there is plenty of free parking for all visitors. **In the second place**, there are luxury hotels, with all the bells and whistles, as well as more economical inns and even campsites for those who like to rough it. **What's more**, there are lots of things to do, from golfing to swimming and other water sports, **plus** many activities organized especially for children. **Finally/For the frosting on the cake/As if that weren't enough/To top it all off**, the fresh air and quiet atmosphere guarantee you an invigorating, yet relaxing, break from city life.

Besides

In a **con** (negative) argument, the same expressions are used, with one exception: instead of **in addition**, **besides** is used.

> I don't recommend the lake district for a family vacation. **In the first place**, it's very expensive for what it offers. **In the second place**, it's just as hot there as it is in the city, and **besides**, the place is full of mosquitoes. **Finally**, the roads that take you there are jammed with traffic all summer. Why not opt for a change of scenery and go a little farther away?

So far

So far indicates what has happened between the beginning of something and the present time. It can go before the subject or at the end of the phrase.

> We have a hundred signatures on the petition **so far**.
> **So far** we have a hundred signatures on the petition.

Still

Still has a number of meanings. Here it indicates that what follows is contrary to and more important than what preceded it.

I would like to have that job. **Still**, it would be very difficult for me to move to another city to be able to do it. (I probably wouldn't accept it if they offered it to me.)

It would be very difficult for me to move to another city to be able to take that job. **Still**, I would like to have it. (I would probably accept it if they offered it to me.)

On the other hand can be used for the same purpose.

I would love to move to a place with a better climate. **On the other hand**, my whole family lives here. (I'll probably stay here.)

My whole family lives here. **On the other hand**, I would love to move to a place with a better climate. (I might move.)

Since

Since has a number of meanings. It can indicate the beginning of a time period that extends to now.

I haven't seen my uncle **since** last Friday.
They've been living in their new house **since** June.

In the example conversation **since** means because, indicating convenience.

I can take you home, **since** your house isn't far from mine.
Since you came early, you can help me finish setting up for the party.

Yikes

Yikes is an expression that indicates surprise—either good or bad.

You have just won a trip for two to Hawaii.	**Yikes!** Wait 'til I tell my husband!
You are charged with driving more than fifteen miles over the speed limit.	**Yikes!** Wait 'til I tell my husband!

Good grief

Good grief is an expression that indicates mild displeasure.

More homework? **Good grief**, Miss Thompson, you've already given us a paper to write!

Just sayin' . . .

Just sayin' . . . is an expression that is intended to subtly show the speaker's desire that you consider something just suggested.

There's a good movie on tonight, and I have a big flat-screen TV. **Just sayin'** . . .
It could be that you're being a little hard on your sister. **Just sayin'** . . .

I mean

I mean introduces an explanation or further comment on what was previously said.

I really don't recommend that teacher! **I mean**, she gives way too much homework.

You guys

You guys is an informal way to address more than one person. In the southern part of the United States, **y'all** is commonly used instead.

> What are **you guys** doing for the Fourth of July?
> What are **y'all** doing for the Fourth of July?

You people is considered extremely insulting. It's best not to use it.

Friction

Friction can mean unrest, difficulty, or disagreement between two or more people.

> You guys have got to learn to get along. There is too much **friction** in this office.

Really

Really can be used in several ways. In the example conversation it indicates agreement with what was said before.

> The new teacher is fantastic. **Really**, she says she will help everybody get an A.

Total

Total, when used as an adjective (before a noun), means complete.

> He's a **total** slob. He never cleans his desk.

Zero

Zero, when used before a noun, means no amount of.

> She's hard to work for. She has **zero** patience.

Squat

Squat means nothing at all.

> I went to every class, and I didn't learn **squat**. It was all a review of the previous class.

Obviously

Obviously indicates that what is going to be said is already known by the listener(s); an alternative is **of course**.

> John's dog just died. **Obviously**, he's feeling sad.

Hardly

Hardly means almost not at all.

> She **hardly** has enough money to live on.

Hardly ever means almost never.

> He **hardly ever** calls his mother.

Not exactly

Not exactly, when used before an adjective, means hardly.

> Well, this is **not exactly** the best pizza I ever ate.

Inside out

Inside out can indicate that an inner surface has become the outer surface.

> You have your shirt on **inside out**.

It can also indicate a thorough knowledge of something.

> Get Pierre to help you with your French. He knows the grammar **inside out**.

Keep on

To **keep on** means to continue or not stop. It is followed by a verb in **-ing** form.

> We can't take a break. We have to **keep on** studying.

Think outside the box

To **think outside the box** means to be creative or to always have new ideas for solving problems.

> When she solved the school's traffic problem, she was really **thinking outside the box**.

Fall off

To **fall off** can mean, literally, to accidentally disappear from a high point.

> He broke his leg when he **fell off** the diving board.

It can also mean to decline or be reduced.

> Sales of new houses began to **fall off** during the month of January.

Put one's two cents in

To **put one's two cents in** means to offer one's opinion.

> Everybody is arguing about this. OK, I'll **put my two cents in**: we should go home and think about this and then try to discuss it calmly next week.

A bit uppity

To be **a bit uppity** means to act as if you were superior to other people. Alternative expressions include **to be stuck-up/to be snooty/to be a snob**.

> Maybe she's just not used to the job, but the new secretary seems to be **a bit uppity**.

Put someone's name up

To **put someone's name up** means to nominate someone for a position or office.

> No, I'm not running for president of the fraternity. I don't know who **put my name up**.

Go along with

To **go along with** means to accept an idea or decision.

> I really don't agree with some of these rules, but I will **go along with** whatever the majority decides.

Handle

To **handle** means to do whatever necessary to perform a duty in a satisfactory way.

> The job is hard, but I think she can **handle** it.

To **handle** can also mean to touch.

> Please do not **handle** the merchandise.

Had better

Had better indicates a warning and implies that if something isn't done, there will be negative consequences. It is usually used in the form of a contraction.

> **They'd better** arrive on time. [Otherwise, they'll miss the bus.]
> **I'd better not** go out tonight. [I have a test tomorrow that I need to study for.]
> **You'd better not** tell anyone my secret. [If you do, I'll be very angry.]

EXERCISE
10·1

Fill in each blank with the word or expression (e.g., in the first place, in the second place, plus, in addition) that best organizes a convincing argument.

1. Man, I'm not going to see that movie.
   a. _____, it's a chick flick.
   b. _____, it's starring Myra Delgado.
   c. _____, it lasts two and a half hours!

2. Girl, I can't wait to see that movie.
   a. _____, it's a chick flick.
   b. _____, it's starring Myra Delgado.
   c. _____, it lasts two and a half hours!

3. This is a house you should consider buying.
   a. _____, it's in a fantastic location.
   b. _____, it's in a great school district.
   c. _____, it has four bedrooms and four bathrooms all on one floor.
   d. _____, the kitchen has been completely updated.
   e. _____, the backyard is private, and there is room for a swimming pool.

Match the words or expressions in the first column with those in the second column that have a similar meaning. Note: There may be more than one match for each expression.

1. _____ keep on

2. _____ fall off

3. _____ handle

4. _____ be uppity

5. _____ go along with

6. _____ put a name up

7. _____ put your two cents in

8. _____ think outside the box

a. accept

b. accidentally drop from a higher place

c. add your opinion

d. be a snob

e. be creative

f. be snooty

g. be stuck-up

h. decline in volume

i. manage

j. nominate

k. not stop

l. suggest someone

m. take care of

n. touch

Circle the word or expression that best completes the following sentences.

1. Don't stop now. You need to _____.
   a. put someone's name up
   b. top it all off
   c. keep on trying
   d. be stuck up

2. We need to work harder to keep our profits from _____.
   a. going along
   b. falling off
   c. handling it
   d. keeping on

3. I'd like to get to know her, but she seems to be _____.
   a. a bit uppity
   b. falling off
   c. thinking outside the box
   d. putting her two cents in

4. This is a big project. Do you think you can _____?
   a. keep on it
   b. top it all off
   c. fall off it
   d. handle it

5. I've heard everybody's opinion except yours. It's time for you to _____.
   a. put your two cents in
   b. think outside the box
   c. handle it
   d. be a bit uppity

6. We need to _____ if we want to compete in today's market.
   a. think outside the box   c. be a bit uppity
   b. top it all off   d. fall off

7. We're in a bit of trouble. Our profits are _____.
   a. inside out   c. stuck-up
   b. falling off   d. topping it all off

8. It's been a bad week. Long days at the office, problems at home, and
   _____, I've come down with the flu.
   a. to go along with that   c. handle that
   b. to put your name up to   d. to top it all off

9. Do you want to be treasurer? I'll _____.
   a. fall off   c. keep on trying
   b. put your name up   d. put your two cents in

10. You think we should get a new car? I'll _____.
    a. think outside the box   c. top it all off
    b. go along with that   d. put your name up

EXERCISE
10·4

Circle the word or expression that best completes each of the following sentences.

1. _____ you're here, you might as well wait.
   a. Good grief   c. Yikes
   b. Really   d. Since

2. It's a beautiful day. Maybe you should take a break and go for a walk
   with me. _____
   a. I mean . . .   c. Still . . .
   b. Just sayin' . . .   d. Furthermore . . .

3. _____! You've been working for nine hours.
   a. Good grief   c. Just sayin' . . .
   b. Since   d. Still

4. I'm ready for a vacation; _____, I haven't had one for more than a year.
   a. Still   c. hardly ever
   b. I mean   d. so far

5. What's the matter? You _____ call me anymore.
   a. still   c. hardly ever
   b. obviously   d. so far

6. How many miles have we driven _____?
   a. hardly   c. so far
   b. squat   d. still

7. You have the flu. _____, you should go home.
   a. Still   c. Obviously
   b. So far   d. Total

8. You paid $200 for a pair of shoes? _____!
   a. Just sayin'...   c. I mean
   b. Yikes   d. Squat

EXERCISE
10·5

Match the words or expressions in the first column with those in the second column that have a similar meaning. Note: There may be more than one match for each expression.

1. _____ pro   a. almost never
2. _____ plus   b. almost not at all
3. _____ so far   c. because
4. _____ since   d. besides
5. _____ hardly   e. complete
6. _____ zero   f. completely
7. _____ total   g. unfriendliness
8. _____ hardly ever   h. expert
9. _____ friction   i. furthermore
10. _____ good grief   j. in addition
11. _____ still   k. it's just a suggestion
12. _____ inside out   l. not exactly
13. _____ just sayin'...   m. of course
14. _____ obviously   n. on the other hand
                                  o. positive characteristic
                                  p. squat
                                  q. until now
                                  r. what's more
                                  s. yikes

Write an appropriate completion to each of the following sentences. Ask an English-speaking friend to check your work.

1. This is a fantastic opportunity. Still, _____.

2. I don't want that job, and besides, _____.

3. He plays the violin professionally. Obviously, _____.

4. Yikes! _____.

5. I'm sad, since you hardly ever _____.

6. I'll go along with _____.

7. My best friend is not exactly _____.

8. I hope no one/someone puts my name up for _____.

9. This is ridiculous, I mean, _____.

10. So far this week, I haven't _____.

Write five sentences indicating what you think you'd better do in order to avoid negative consequences. Indicate what those consequences would be. Use the following sentence as a model. Ask an English-speaking friend to check your work.

I'd better go to bed early tonight; otherwise, I'll be too sleepy to do well on my exam.

_____

_____

_____

_____

_____

Write a convincing argument about a topic that you feel strongly about. Use at least ten of the words or expressions explained in this chapter. Ask an English-speaking friend to check your work.

_____

_____

_____

_____

_____

_____

_____

_____

_____

_____

Narrating a story

11

Conversation: A traffic accident

JACK: Hey, buddy, what happened to you? Don't tell me you broke your leg!

SAM: No, it's not that drastic. I just twisted my ankle. Still, it hurts a lot, and walking with these crutches is a **pain in the neck**.

JACK: So when did it happen?

SAM: It was the night of the basketball championship. And **the worst thing** is that we lost the game and all hopes of winning our title back.

JACK: What a **bummer**! Sit down here for a minute and tell me all about it.

SAM: Well, it all happened last Thursday. It was **pouring down rain** and also freezing. I was in a hurry to get to the gym early to **chill out** a bit before the game. I was all **stressed out** about the game when I left home, but I got in the car and started to drive toward the gym. **All of a sudden** my phone rang—it was my girlfriend. She was **all excited** about the game and wanted to **wish** me good luck. I started to get **pumped up** and ready for the game. My girlfriend and I kept on talking when I suddenly **realized** that the cars in front of me were stopped, and I was going a little fast. I slammed on the brakes, but it was **too** late. The street was wet, and I hit the car that was stopped **in front of** me. That hard braking caused me to twist my ankle. I could hardly get out of the car to talk to the other driver because my ankle hurt so much. **To tell you the truth**, I was so **freaked out** I didn't know what to do. I was thinking about the game, my girlfriend, my teammates—it never occurred to me that I wouldn't be able to play that night. **Finally** a **cop** came and made me sign some **papers**; then an ambulance took me to the hospital. They took some X-rays to see if my ankle was broken or not. **Thank goodness** it wasn't broken, but **the upshot** was that I wasn't going to play basketball that night. And now I'm **stuck with** these crutches.

Improving your conversation

The example dialogue is very informal and uses only a few of the traditional markers that indicate the order of events in a narration.

First/second/next/then/after that

In a more formal or longer narration, chronological order can be made clearer with the use of expressions such as **first**, **second**, **next**, **then**, and **after that**. The last event in the series is preceded by **finally**.

> **First**, I got into the car and started to drive toward the gym.
> **Second**, I had an accident.
> **Then** I realized that I had twisted my ankle.

After that, they took me to the hospital.
Finally, I went to the game on crutches and watched my team lose.

Note that each of these expressions is followed by a comma (or pause, when speaking), with the exception of **then**. **Second** can be replaced with **then**, **next**, or **after that**, which are interchangeable.

This is what happened at the meeting this afternoon. **First**, we discussed the budget; **second**, the chairman announced the new position in Human Services. **Next** we talked about the problems in Customer Service. **After that**, we had a short coffee break, and **then** we had a chance to ask questions. **Finally**, we adjourned.

Finally

Finally can also indicate relief or joy that something long awaited or expected has happened.

After three long days on the road, I **finally** got to San Antonio.
Finally you're here! We expected you two hours ago.

Thank goodness

Thank goodness and **thank God** are other ways to express relief, joy, or satisfaction.

Thank goodness you arrived safely. Now we can celebrate.

Thank goodness and **thank God** (but not **finally**) can also express appreciation.

We have enough money to live on, **thank God**.
All of the children are healthy, **thank goodness**.

To top it all off

Sometimes a series of events are meant to tell a convincing story. **To top it all off** is an expression that is used to introduce a final event that adds weight to the sum of the previous events. Other expressions with the same function are **for the frosting on the cake** and **as if that weren't enough**.

First, my alarm didn't go off, and I woke up an hour late. **Then** I spilled coffee all over my suit and had to change clothes. **After that**, I got in the car and noticed that it was completely out of gas. **Finally**, I had to wait in a long line to get gas. And **to top it all off**, when I left the gas station, I was in the middle of a huge traffic jam.

All of a sudden

Events that interrupt a narration can be preceded by **all of a sudden, suddenly, before I knew it, out of nowhere, out of the blue,** and **just like that**—all of which mean without warning.

We were enjoying our picnic, when **all of a sudden**, it began to rain cats and dogs.
They were taking a test, when **suddenly** the fire alarm went off.
I stepped on a slippery rock, and **before I knew it**, I was on the ground.
He was driving down the street, and **out of nowhere**, a car approached from the left.
I was watching TV the other night, when **out of the blue** I got a call from an old friend whom I hadn't seen in ages.
I was feeling a little depressed, and **just like that**, my favorite song came on the radio and cheered me up.

The best thing and the worst thing

The best thing and **the worst thing** indicate that what follows is the most or least desirable aspect of an issue.

> **The best thing** about this school is that it has wonderful students. They are all eager to learn.
> **The best thing** you can do at this point is be patient.
> **The worst thing** about this apartment is the location. It's not convenient to anything.

The upshot

The upshot of an issue is its result or outcome. This is often used to avoid telling a complete story or explaining an issue in detail.

> I'm not going to give you all the details. **The upshot** is that Caitlyn has left town and won't be back.

An expression that has a similar function is **the bottom line**.

> I just had a long conversation with the chairman of the company. **The bottom line** is that I've been promoted.

> I don't have time to hear your whole story—what's **the bottom line**?

> **The bottom line** is that I got fired and I'm looking for a new job.

Paper

Paper has a number of meanings. **Paper** is the most common material used for writing, printing, and cleaning, and it is in many manufactured goods. In this function, it is a non-count noun and is not made plural.

> This book is made of **paper**.
> We need to conserve **paper** in order to protect our forests.

Paper can also be a count noun, and can be made plural, when it means document.

> We need to fill out a whole bunch of **papers** when we go to the doctor.

Paper is also a count noun when it means essay, written composition, or thesis.

> I have two research **papers** to write, so I will probably spend the weekend in the library.

A **paper** can refer to the newspaper. **The paper** can mean today's newspaper.

> She went down to the newsstand to buy a **paper**.
> Have you read **the paper** yet? The news is amazing!

Bummer

A **bummer** is an item of bad news or bad luck.

> Snow again! What a **bummer**! Now our flight will be canceled.

For serious occasions or tragedies, **a shame** would be a better expression.

> I'm so sorry to hear about your dad's illness. What **a shame**!

Pain in the neck

A **pain in the neck** can refer to anything or any person that is annoying.

> I wish my sister would stop banging on the door. She really is a **pain in the neck**.
> I lost my Internet connection again. What a **pain in the neck**!

Cop

Cop is a slang term that means police officer.

> There are **cops** stationed along the turnpike, waiting for speeders.

To **cop out on someone** has nothing to do with the police; it means to stop participating in an activity in which other people are counting on you. It indicates that the speaker is unhappy with this decision.

> We had five players for the basketball team, but Steve **copped out**, and now we can't play a proper game.
> Sandy promised to drive me to the game, but he **copped out on me** at the last minute, so now I'll have to take the bus.

Pouring down rain

To be **pouring down rain** means to be raining heavily. An alternative expression is **raining cats and dogs**.

> The kids can't play outside; it's **pouring down rain**.
> I had to pull the car off to the side of the road because it was **raining cats and dogs**.

Pumped up

To be **pumped (up)** means to be excited. An alternative expression is to be **all excited**.

> We are both **pumped up** for the concert this weekend.
> She is **all excited** about her date with you. Where are you guys going?

Stressed out

To be **stressed out** means to be very tense, nervous, or worried about something.

> She has two sick children at home and is trying to work at the same time. No wonder she is **stressed out**!

Another way to express this feeling is to say that something **stresses you out**.

> Having two sick children at home really **stresses me out**.

Freaked out

To **freak out** or be **freaked out** means to be extremely scared, angry, or excited. Also, something can **freak you out**.

> He **freaked out** when he saw his brother driving his new car.
> She is **freaked out** because she has three exams tomorrow.
> That car speeding toward us really **freaked me out**.

Creeped out

To be **creeped out** means to be disgusted or frightened by something. Also, something can **creep you out**.

> Those pictures of dead bodies really **creeped me out**.
> It **creeps me out** that he just sits there and never says a word.

Another way to indicate disgust is to be **grossed out**.

> It really **grosses me out** when the kids have food fights.

Stuck with

To be **stuck with** means to have to cope with an uncomfortable or undesirable situation.

> My brother went out with his friends, and I'm **stuck with** looking after my little sister.

Chill out

To **chill out** means to relax or calm down.

> Come on over! We're just **chillin' out** on the back patio.
> Oooh! I'm so mad I could scream!   **Chill out**, babe. It's not worth getting upset over.

Realize

To **realize** means to be aware of, to already know.

> I'm sorry I yelled at you. I **realize** that I was wrong.

Wish

To **wish** means to be sorry that something isn't true. It is followed by a clause with a subjunctive verb.

> [You are not here.] I **wish** you were here.
> [I can't go with you.] I **wish** I could go with you.

Wish is also used in formal greetings.

> We **wish** you a happy New Year.
> I **wish** you the best of luck.

To tell you the truth

To tell you the truth precedes information that may surprise the listener.

> Did you enjoy your trip?   **To tell you the truth**, it wasn't that great.

Too

Too has a number of meanings. It can mean also.

> I went home early, and Jon did, **too**.

It can mean excessively.

> She is way **too** thin. I'm afraid she's anorexic.

It can mean so extreme that there is a negative result.

> He has **too** much free time. He gets into trouble.
> She's **too** nice. It creeps me out.

In front of

In front of indicates the location of something in relation to something else. It can mean facing something else.

> The teacher sat in a chair **in front of** her students and read them a story.

It can mean ahead of, facing in the same direction as, something else.

> There were three cars **in front of** mine, waiting for the light.
> I had to stand in line, and there were a lot of people **in front of** me.

It can mean within someone's eyesight, facing in any direction.

> There is a car parked on the street **in front of** your house.

EXERCISE
11·1

Fill in each blank with the word or expression (e.g., first, next, then, finally, etc.) that best emphasizes the chronological order of the following sentences.

1. a. _____, I walked into the classroom. b. _____ I sat down. c. _____, I opened my book and started to study. d. _____, the teacher came in and gave us the test.

2. It was a wonderful day. a. _____, I had breakfast in bed. b. _____. I took a long shower and got dressed. c. _____, my boyfriend came over and took me downtown. We went to two museums and d. _____ did some shopping. e. _____, he brought me back home. f. _____, when I walked in the door, all my friends and family were there to give me a surprise birthday party!

EXERCISE
11·2

Circle the word or expression that most appropriately completes each sentence.

1. After five years of studying, he _____ got his degree.
   a. just like that   c. finally
   b. suddenly   d. after that

2. It's been dry all summer long, and now, _____ it's pouring down rain.
   a. thank goodness   c. the bottom line is
   b. before you know it   d. to top it all off

3. She was going to help us, but she _____.
   a. was pumped up
   b. chilled out
   c. copped out
   d. realized

4. I wanted to go with them, but I was _____.
   a. all excited
   b. a pain in the neck
   c. a bummer
   d. too late

5. The insects in that horror movie really _____.
   a. creeped me out
   b. chilled me out
   c. gave me a pain in the neck
   d. rained cats and dogs

EXERCISE
11·3

Match the words and expressions in the first column with those in the second column that have a similar meaning. Note: There may be more than one match for each expression.

1. _____ after that

2. _____ first

3. _____ suddenly

4. _____ upshot

5. _____ paper

6. _____ bummer

7. _____ pain in the neck

8. _____ cop

9. _____ in front of

10. _____ to top it all off

a. across from

b. ahead of

c. all of a sudden

d. annoying

e. as if that weren't enough

f. bad luck

g. bad news

h. before anything else happened

i. before I knew it

j. bottom line

k. document

l. essay

m. facing

n. for the frosting on the cake

o. in sight of

p. just like that

q. material to write on

r. newspaper

s. next

t. out of nowhere

u. out of the blue

v.   police officer

w.   result

x.   second

y.   then

EXERCISE 11·4

Write an appropriate question or remark for each of the following responses. Ask an English-speaking friend to check your answers.

1. _____

What a bummer!

2. _____

He's a real pain in the neck.

3. _____

Thank goodness, we're all safe.

4. _____

I finished writing it last night, thank God.

5. _____

Yeah, that's the bottom line.

6. _____

It was right out of the blue.

EXERCISE 11·5

Match the words or expressions in the first column with those in the second column that have a similar meaning. Note: There may be more than one match for each expression.

1. _____ be pumped up   a.   be all excited

2. _____ be stuck with   b.   be angry

3. _____ be raining cats and dogs   c.   be aware of

4. _____ be freaked out   d.   be disgusted

5. _____ be stressed out   e.   be frightened

6. _____ chill out   f.   be grossed out

7. _____ realize

8. _____ be creeped out

9. _____ wish

10. _____ cop out

g. be in an unfortunate situation

h. be nervous

i. be pouring down rain

j. be scared

k. be sorry that something isn't true

l. be surprised

m. be tense

n. be worried

o. calm down

p. feel enthusiastic

q. know

r. not participate as promised

s. relax

t. stop worrying

Write an appropriate question or remark for each response. Ask an English-speaking friend to check your work.

1. _____

That really creeps me out.

2. _____

You need to chill out.

3. _____

They copped out on me.

4. _____

I realize that.

5. _____

No wonder you're stressed out!

EXERCISE 11·7

Form sentences beginning with I wish *to indicate your regret that the previous information is not true.*

1. You are not here.

   _____

2. I can't get a promotion at this company.

   _____

3. She is always stressed out.

   _____

4. He doesn't know my e-mail address.

   _____

5. They never come to see me.

   _____

EXERCISE 11·8

Circle the most appropriate answer for each question or remark.

1. How was your interview?
   a. It was pouring down rain.
   b. It was the worst thing.
   c. It was out of nowhere.
   d. To tell you the truth, it stressed me out.

2. What's the matter?
   a. I'm stuck with the job of collecting money.
   b. I have a pain in the neck.
   c. To tell you the truth, that's the upshot.
   d. The best thing is that she copped out.

3. My dog died yesterday.
   a. What a pain in the neck.
   b. What a shame.
   c. It's raining cats and dogs.
   d. To top it all off, I'm chilling out.

4. Tell me what happened.
   a. I'm out of paper.
   b. That creeps me out.
   c. The upshot is that I'm single again.
   d. It's a good paper.

5. A strange person calls me in the middle of the night and then hangs up.
   a. That chills me out.
   b. That grosses me out.
   c. That creeps me out.
   d. That's a cop-out.

EXERCISE
11·9

Have you ever been freaked out? Write four or five sentences to describe what happened. Ask an English-speaking friend to check your work.

_____

_____

_____

_____

_____

_____

EXERCISE
11·10

Write a narration that describes something that happened recently in your life. Use at least eight of the words or expressions explained in this chapter. Ask an English-speaking friend to check your work.

_____

_____

_____

_____

_____

_____

_____

_____

_____

_____

_____

_____

Retelling a conversation ·12·

Conversation A: In the present tense

MIKE: Hey **dude**, what's up? I hear you have a new job. **How's it going?**

ADAM: **Pretty well**, so far. I have a lot to learn, but the people are nice, and there's not too much **pressure**.

MIKE: What do you do?

ADAM: Basically, I'm **learning the ropes** of management, studying the history of the company so I know how everything works.

MIKE: That's great! I hope it all works out for you.

MIKE (retelling the conversation): I asked Adam what **was** up and told him that I **heard** he **had** a new job. I asked him how it **was** going. He told me that it **was** going pretty well, so far. He said that he **had** a lot to learn but that the people **were** nice and that there **wasn't** too much pressure. Then I asked him what he **did**. He answered that basically he **was learning the ropes** of management and studying the history of the company so that he **knew** how everything **worked**. Then I told him that that **was** great and that I **hoped** it **worked** out for him.

Conversation B: In the present perfect tense

RENEE: Have you eaten yet?

EMILY: No, but **I've already bought** my lunch. Want to join me in the park?

RENEE: Thanks, but **I've made** a reservation for two at Kincaid's Restaurant. **Have** you **ever eaten** there?

EMILY: Yes, **I've been** there several times. It's great!

RENEE (retelling the conversation): I asked Emily if she **had eaten** yet, and she told me that she **had** already **bought** her lunch. She asked me if I **wanted** to join her in the park, but I told her that I **had made** a reservation for two at Kincaid's Restaurant. Then I asked her if she **had ever eaten** there, and she told me yes, that she **had been** there several times. She said it **was** great.

Conversation C: In the past tense

JASON: Where were you last night? We missed you at the party.

GINA: Oh, I had to go to my sister's house. They called her from the hospital **at the last minute** and asked her to work the night shift, so I went over to **babysit** for her kids. I **ended up** spending the night at her place.

JASON (retelling the conversation): I asked Gina where she **had been** the night before and told her that we **had missed** her at the party. She said that she **had had** to go to her sister's house—that they **had called** her sister from the hospital at the last minute and **had asked** her to work the night shift, so she **had gone** over to **babysit** for her kids. She said she **had ended up** spending the night at her sister's place.

Less formal:

JASON (retelling the conversation): I asked Gina where she **was** the night before and told her that we **missed** her at the party. She said that she **had** to go to her sister's house—that they **called** her sister from the hospital at the last minute and **asked** her to work the night shift, so she **went** over to **babysit** for her kids. She said she **ended up** spending the night at her sister's place.

Conversation D: In future tenses

BEN: Hi, Jeremy. What are you guys doing tonight? I'm kind of **at a loose end** since I broke up with Sydney.

JEREMY: Join us, then—we're going to hang out downtown—probably go to several places. Are you up for that?

BEN: Definitely. Where should I meet you? Better still, can you **give me a ride**?

JEREMY: Glad to. I'll **pick you up** at your place at 9:30. OK?

BEN: Perfect. I'll look out for you.

BEN (retelling the conversation): I said hi to Jeremy and asked him what he and the other guys were doing that night. I told him that I had been kind of **at a loose end** ever since I broke up with Sydney. He told me to join them and said that they were going to hang out downtown—probably go to several places. He asked me if I was up for that. I said that I definitely was and asked him where I should meet them. Then I told him that it would be even better if he could **give me a ride**. He said he would be glad to and told me that he would **pick me up** at my place at 9:30. He asked me if that would be OK. I said that it would be perfect and that I would look out for him.

Improving your conversation

Using the present perfect tense

The present perfect tense is used to indicate experience that relates to the present time.

The present perfect tense is formed by a conjugation of the verb *have* followed by the past participle form of the main verb.

The past participle form of most verbs is the same form as the past tense form.

Present tense	Past tense	Past participle
call	called	**called**
catch	caught	**caught**
hit	hit	**hit**
join	joined	**joined**
kick	kicked	**kicked**
like	liked	**liked**
love	loved	**loved**
teach	taught	**taught**
walk	walked	**walked**
work	worked	**worked**

However, many frequently used verbs have irregular past participle forms. Several examples follow. Check Appendix A for a complete list.

be	was/were	**been**
do	did	**done**
eat	ate	**eaten**
give	gave	**given**
see	saw	**seen**
take	took	**taken**

Expressions often used with the present perfect tense include the following:

Already

Already means at some time in the past and can indicate that the action does not need to be repeated.

> I'm not hungry. I've **already** eaten.
> You don't need to close the windows—we've **already** done it.

Already can be used in a question, indicating surprise that something has been done.

> Have you finished high school **already**? (I can't believe you are old enough!)

Yet

Yet can be used in a question to find out if something has been done.

> Have you eaten **yet**?
> Have you taken the test **yet**?

Not yet

Not yet is used to indicate that something has not been done—and that it should be done in the future.

> We're hungry. We have**n't** eaten **yet**.
> I'm not finished traveling. I have**n't** been to Africa **yet**.

So far

So far means as of this date or time.

> She has come to class on time every day, **so far**.
> How many continents have you been to?   **So far**, I've only been to North and South America.

Ever

Ever means at any time in the past or future. It is placed between the modal verb and the main verb.

> Have you **ever** been in California?
> I won't **ever** do that again.

Ever can be used after *never* to emphasize its meaning.

> He was never, **ever**, there.

Modal verbs

Modal verbs have past tense forms, as follows:

Present tense	Past tense
can (ability/permission)	**could**
may (permission)	**could**
may (possibility)	**may have** + past participle
might (possibility)	**might have** + past participle
should (obligation/advisability)	**should have** + past participle
have to/must (necessity)	**had to**
must (probability)	**must have** + past participle
will (regularity/reliability)	**would**

When I was a teenager, I **could** do backflips.
When you were in high school, **could** you stay out late?
I don't know where she is. She **may/might have gone** to the store.
You **should have been** here last night. It was a great party.
Sorry I couldn't make it—I **had to** work.
He's really late. He **must have gotten** stuck in a traffic jam.
He **would** come over and say hello every morning.
I called his cell phone, so that he **would** wake up.

Direct and indirect discourse

A retold conversation is also called indirect discourse. Verbs that indicate what someone communicates to another include *say, tell, indicate, explain, shout, yell, complain, cry, whisper, promise*, and others. There are certain patterns for indirect discourse.

Pattern 1: Present tense + any other tense

When the communicating verb is in the present tense, the second verb is in its normal tense. This indicates that the speaker continues to affirm belief in what follows.

Joe: I **buy** French bread and cheese every Sunday morning.
Joe **says** (that) he **buys** French bread and cheese every Sunday morning.

Joe: I **have bought** French bread every Sunday morning for five years.
Joe **says** (that) he **has bought** French bread every Sunday morning for five years.

Joe: I **bought** French bread last Sunday.
Joe **says** (that) he **bought** French bread last Sunday.

Joe: I **will buy** French bread next Sunday.
Joe **says** (that) he **will buy** French bread next Sunday.

Pattern 2: Past tense + a previous tense

When the communicating verb is in the past tense, the second verb is in a previous tense, as follows:

present → past   Note that the meaning is still in present time.
Joe: I **buy** French bread and cheese every Sunday morning.
Joe **said** (that) he **bought** French bread and cheese every Sunday morning.
(Joe buys French bread and cheese every Sunday morning.)

present perfect → past perfect
Joe: I **have bought** French bread every Sunday morning for five years.
Joe **said** (that) he **had bought** French bread every Sunday morning for five years.

past → past perfect
Joe: I **bought** French bread last Sunday.
Joe **said** (that) he **had bought** French bread last Sunday.

future → conditional
Joe: I **will buy** French bread next Sunday.
Joe **said** (that) he **would buy** French bread next Sunday.

Indirect yes-or-no questions use pattern 2 plus the word *if*.

Maria: Are you going out?
Maria **asked** me **if** I **was going** out.

Ben: Have you bought the bread?
Ben **asked** if I **had bought** the bread.

Ben: Did you buy the wine?
Ben **asked** if I **had bought** the wine.

Ben: Will you bring the wine next Sunday?
Ben **asked** if I **would bring** the wine next Sunday.

Indirect information questions use pattern 2 plus the appropriate question word (*who/when/where/why/what/how/*etc.).

Alex: What time does the movie start?
Alex **asked** me **what time** the movie started.

Kevin: What have you done?
Kevin **asked** me **what** I **had done.**

Cathy: Where did they go?
Cathy **asked** her **where** they had gone.

Charles: How long will the surgery take?
Charles **asked how long** the surgery **would** take.

Dude

Dude is a very informal way to address a male friend.

Hey, **dude**—what's up?

How's it going?

How's it going? is an informal greeting. It's often answered with **pretty well**.

Hi, Ethan. **How's it going?**
Pretty well, thanks. How are you?

At the last minute

At the last minute indicates that something happened immediately before it was too late.

The man picked up his tickets **at the last minute**—just before the show started.

Pressure

Pressure refers to the stress of responsibility people feel when too many things are expected of them at the same time.

> It's hard to ever relax. I have so much **pressure** at work—and with two small children, there's **pressure** at home, too.

Learning the ropes

To be **learning the ropes** means to be getting acquainted with a new job or routine.

> There's a lot of pressure at first, but once you **learn the ropes**, you'll be fine.

At a loose end

To be **at a loose end** means to temporarily not have anything to do or not know what to do.

> Would you like me to paint your room? I'm **at** a bit of **a loose end**.

End up

To **end up** means to find one's self doing something unplanned or in an unexpected situation.

> I fell asleep on the train and **ended up** in New Jersey.
> She worked here as a temporary secretary and **ended up** getting a full-time job with the company.

Babysit

To **babysit** means to **take care of** or **look after** someone else's children.

> She makes extra money **babysitting** on weekends.
> Will you **take care of** the baby for a couple of hours?
> I hope you can **look after** the kids while I go to the store.

Give someone a ride

To **give someone a ride** means to offer to take someone somewhere in your car or other vehicle.

> I see you missed the bus. If you like, I'll **give you a ride** home.

Pick up

To **pick up** means to go in a vehicle to where someone is waiting, for the purpose of giving him or her a ride.

> I'll be glad to give you a ride. I'll **pick you up** in front of the school.

Circle the word or expression that best completes each of the following sentences.

1. You were here yesterday? Then you've seen the new office _____!
   a. already   c. ever
   b. yet   d. so far

2. Have you _____ eaten at M Zapp's restaurant?
   a. already   c. ever
   b. yet   d. so far

3. No, I haven't been there _____.
   a. already   c. ever
   b. yet   d. so far

4. You have to take five tests? How many have you taken _____?
   a. already   c. ever
   b. yet   d. so far

5. She has never, _____, taken a bribe.
   a. already   c. ever
   b. yet   d. so far

6. My mom can't wait to get here. She hasn't seen the baby _____.
   a. already   c. ever
   b. yet   d. so far

7. Don't worry about the tickets. I've _____ bought them.
   a. already   c. ever
   b. yet   d. so far

8. Tell me, have my packages arrived _____?
   a. already   c. ever
   b. yet   d. so far

Fill in each blank with the present perfect form of the indicated verb and the adverb, if mentioned.

1. She _____ (take) only half of her medicine.

2. I _____ (read) that book twice.

3. You _____ (finish, not) your dinner yet.

4. We _____ (register, already) for the class.

5. So far, they _____ (call) us four times.

6. He _____ (be, never) in this house.

7. I _____ (see, not) a good movie in a long time.

8. _____ (you, do) your homework yet?

9. They _____ (buy, already) a new car.

10. _____ (she, go) to Florida yet?

EXERCISE
12·3

Convert the following sentences from the present tense to the past tense, changing the wording where necessary for them to make sense.

1. Now he can run a mile in four minutes.

   Last year _____.

2. This year we can take an hour off for lunch.

   Last year _____.

3. It may rain this afternoon.

   _____ last night, but I'm not sure.

4. He might have the flu.

   _____ last week.

5. You should pay your bills on time.

   _____ last month.

6. What should I say when I see him?

   _____ yesterday?

7. We have to rearrange the furniture so the piano will fit.

   _____

8. The children pick the wildflowers every spring.

   _____

9. It must be nine o'clock now.

   _____ then.

10. She's leaving because she has to pick up her daughter.

   _____

Change the following direct quotes to indirect discourse.

1. Scott: I'm leaving for the beach tomorrow.

   Scott said _____.

2. Eric: The train always arrives on time.

   Eric said _____.

3. Adam: We have already eaten lunch.

   Adam said _____.

4. Jack: The plane took off at 9:15.

   Jack said _____.

5. Val: We'll be there in about five minutes.

   Val said _____.

Change the following questions from direct discourse to indirect discourse.

1. My neighbor: Do you have a shovel I can borrow?

   My neighbor asked me _____.

2. Jan: Will you help me with these packages?

   Jan asked the man _____.

3. Laura: What movie are you going to see?

   Laura asked us _____.

4. Thomas: Why did you call?

   Thomas asked him _____.

5. Renee: Who are you talking to?

   Renee asked her _____.

6. Mike: How far is it?

   Mike asked _____.

7. Jason: Do you speak English?

   Jason asked him _____.

8. Sydney: When will you come back?

   Sydney asked me _____.

9. April: Where do you go to school?

   April asked her _____.

10. Holly: Do you want me to help you?

    Holly asked him _____.

Fill in each blank with an appropriate word or expression explained in this chapter.

1. We were going to leave without him, but he arrived _____, thank goodness.

2. This is our receptionist's first day on the job, so she's just _____.

3. Listen, _____, my car broke down, so I don't think I can _____ home this afternoon.

4. I had to leave that company because I was under too much _____.

5. I was _____, so I decided to call up my old friend and invite him over.

6. Hey, dude, _____?

7. The kids are sick, so we won't need you to _____ tonight.

8. Every time I take on a new project, I _____ doing it full-time.

Make a list of ten things that you do every day. Then write a sentence that tells which of these things you have already done. After that, write a sentence that tells which of these things you haven't done yet. Ask an English-speaking friend to check your sentences.

_____

_____

_____

_____

_____

_____

_____

_____

_____

_____

Listen to a conversation of eight to ten lines between two people, and write down exactly what they say. Then change the direct quotes to indirect discourse. If live conversations are too fast for you to write down, try copying a conversation from a television program that you can replay as needed. Ask an English-speaking friend to check your work.

_____

_____

_____

_____

_____

_____

_____

_____

Electronic conversation ·13·

While face-to-face conversations are still considered to be the best ones, people everywhere are depending more and more on electronic devices for communication. Apart from the fixed telephone, which has been around since 1876—and is still going strong—conversations are now also carried on through cell phones, e-mail, and other electronic devices.

E-mail

E-mail (electronic mail) enables written conversations that are either typed on a computer or cell phone keyboard or entered on a touch screen on a cell phone or other electronic device. These messages are then sent to the desired recipient via the Internet. In order to use **e-mail**, you need to have an **e-mail address**, and you need to know the **e-mail address** of the person with whom you wish to communicate.

E-mail addresses can be assigned by the company that provides an Internet connection or through companies that issue subscriptions through the Internet. An **e-mail address** begins with a series of numbers or letters (of the individual's choosing), followed by the symbol @ (pronounced "at"), and then followed by the name of the provider, a period (pronounced "dot"), and finally a suffix of two or three more letters that indicates the domain—the type of organization that is providing the **e-mail account**. Here are some examples of these final domain letters:

com	commercial (the most widely used suffix; preferred by businesses)
edu	education (for schools, colleges, and universities)
gov	government (for government organizations)
net	network (most commonly used by Internet service providers)
org	organization (primarily used by nonprofit groups and trade associations)

The suffix can alternatively indicate the name of the source country. For example:

au	Australia
es	Spain
mx	Mexico
uk	United Kingdom

IM

An **IM** is an "instant message," designed to get the immediate attention of the person contacted. Electronic devices give an audible signal when an **IM** is received.

Texting

Texting is the practice of sending written messages from one cell phone to another, using the receiver's telephone number.

Texters often leave out the vowels in words or make up abbreviations in order to communicate faster. For example:

cd	could
cls	class
cn	can
hv	have
prnts	parents
sndy	Sunday
tchr	teacher
wd	would

Tweeting

Tweeting is the practice of sending written messages to the general public through a commercial website, called twitter.com. Messages are limited to 140 characters. Important or famous people often use this to keep their constituents, clients, or fans informed of what they are doing or thinking.

Acronyms

Acronyms are combinations of letters that are used as abbreviations to replace words and expressions. **Acronyms** and other symbols are commonly used in **e-mail**, **texting**, and **tweeting**. They may be in all capital (uppercase) letters, all lowercase letters, or a combination of the two. There are really no rules!

Following is a list of commonly used **acronyms** and other symbols:

☺, :)	I'm happy.
☹, :(	I'm unhappy.
@	at
2nite	tonight
4	for/four
411	information [traditionally a telephone number to call to get help finding a telephone number]
4ever	forever
4U	for you
911	emergency; call me [traditionally the contact number for the police or fire department]
ABT2	about to
AKA	also known as (another name for someone or something)
asamof	as a matter of fact

ASAP	as soon as possible
AWOL	absent without leave (not being where one is supposed to be) [traditionally a military expression]
AYS	are you serious? (really?)
BBB	boring beyond belief
B/C	because
B4	before
B4N	bye for now
BFF	best friends forever
BTDT	been there, done that (I don't need to do it again)
BTW	by the way
BYOB	bring your own beer/bring your own bottle
CEO	chief executive officer [traditionally used to indicate the person in charge of a company]
DIY	do it yourself
DOA	dead on arrival [traditionally used by hospital emergency rooms]
DUI	driving under the influence (of alcohol or drugs) [traditionally used by police departments]
DWI	driving while intoxicated (by alcohol or drugs) [traditionally used by police departments]
ETA	estimated time of arrival [traditionally used in airports and train and bus stations]
EZ	easy
FAQ	frequently asked questions
FF	friends
FSBO	for sale by owner [traditionally used in the real estate industry]
FYI	for your information
GAL	get a life (don't be so boring!)
GO	get out (that's unbelievable!)
GR8	great!
HAND	have a nice day
IM	instant messaging
IMO	in my opinion
ISO	in search of (looking for)
L8R	later
LOL	laugh out loud (what you sent me was funny!)
LTR	long-term relationship
MIA	missing in action [traditionally a military term]
MYOB	mind your own business
N/A	not applicable [traditionally used in formal applications]
NP	no problem
NTW	not to worry (don't worry!)
NW	no way

OBO	or best offer [traditionally used in "for sale" ads]
OK	okay
OMG	oh my God! (also spelled "omigod")
OTC	over the counter (medicine that can be purchased without a doctor's prescription)
OTL	out to lunch (not focused/lacking good judgment)
PC	politically correct (avoiding the use of stereotypes or negative attacks in public)
PC	personal computer
PDA	public display of affection (kissing and hugging in public)
PDQ	pretty damn quick [traditionally a military term]
PLZ	please
POV	point of view (opinion)
PS	postscript [traditionally used after a signature in a letter to add one more message]
R&R	rest and relaxation [traditionally a military term]
RSVP	*répondez s'il vous plaît* (please reply to this invitation)
RUS	are you serious? (really?)
SO	significant other (the other person in a romantic relationship)
SOW	speaking of which
SRO	standing room only [traditionally used in the theater]
TBA	to be advised/announced
TBD	to be determined
TGIF	thank goodness it's Friday
TLC	tender loving care [traditionally used for nurses]
TTYL	talk to you later
TX	thanks
U	you
U2	you, too
UR	you are
W/	with
W/O	without
W8	wait
XOXO	kisses and hugs [traditionally used in written letters: *X* = a kiss; *O* = a hug]
Y	why
YR	yeah right

"Translate" each of the following messages.

1. Cn U cm ovr asap?

   _____

2. AYS? im @schl. BBB

   _____

3. its OVR btwn us. sory

   _____

4. lol UR crzy

   _____

5. im :(w/o U

   _____

6. me2

   _____

7. CU L8r

   _____

8. OMG shes OTL

   _____

Write a text message conversation between you and a good friend. Use at least ten acronyms, symbols, or other abbreviations. Ask an English-speaking friend to check your work.

   _____

   _____

   _____

   _____

   _____

   _____

   _____

   _____

   _____

   _____

   _____

   _____

APPENDIX A

Irregular past tense and past participle forms

Following are common verbs that have irregular past tense forms. Usually the past participle forms are the same as the past tense forms. Those that are *not* are in bold type.

Verb	Past tense	Past participle
be	was/were	**been**
beat	beat	**beaten**
become	became	**become**
begin	began	**begun**
bend	bent	bent
bet	bet	bet
bite	bit	**bitten**
bleed	bled	bled
blow	blew	**blown**
break	broke	**broken**
bring	brought	brought
build	built	built
buy	bought	bought
catch	caught	caught
choose	chose	**chosen**
come	came	**come**
cost	cost	cost
cut	cut	cut
dig	dug	dug
do	did	**done**
draw	drew	**drawn**
drink	drank	**drunk**
drive	drove	**driven**
eat	ate	**eaten**
fall	fell	**fallen**
feed	fed	fed
feel	felt	felt
fight	fought	fought

Verb	Past tense	Past participle
find	found	found
fit	fit	fit
fly	flew	**flown**
forget	forgot	**forgotten**
forgive	forgave	**forgiven**
freeze	froze	**frozen**
get	got	**gotten**
give	gave	**given**
go	went	**gone**
grow	grew	**grown**
hang	hung	hung
have	had	had
hear	heard	heard
hide	hid	**hidden**
hit	hit	hit
hold	held	held
hurt	hurt	hurt
keep	kept	kept
know	knew	**known**
lay	laid	laid
lead	led	led
leave	left	left
lend	lent	lent
let	let	let
lie	lay	**lain**
light	lit	lit
lose	lost	lost
make	made	made
mean	meant	meant
meet	met	met
pay	paid	paid
put	put	put
quit	quit	quit
read	read (pronounced "red")	read (pronounced "red")
ride	rode	**ridden**
ring	rang	**rung**
rise	rose	**risen**
run	ran	**run**
say	said	said
see	saw	**seen**
sell	sold	sold

Verb	Past tense	Past participle
send	sent	sent
set	set	set
shake	shook	**shaken**
shoot	shot	shot
show	showed	**shown**
shrink	shrank	**shrunk**
shut	shut	shut
sing	sang	**sung**
sit	sat	sat
sleep	slept	slept
speak	spoke	**spoken**
speed	sped	sped
spend	spent	spent
spin	spun	spun
spread	spread	spread
stand	stood	stood
steal	stole	**stolen**
sting	stung	stung
strike	struck	struck
sweep	swept	swept
swim	swam	**swum**
take	took	**taken**
teach	taught	taught
tear	tore	torn
tell	told	told
think	thought	thought
throw	threw	**thrown**
understand	understood	understood
upset	upset	upset
wake up	woke up	**woken up**
wear	wore	worn
win	won	won
write	wrote	**written**

APPENDIX B
Short tag questions and answers

Present tense
Be

Questions	Affirmative answers	Negative answers
I am, **am I not**? (formal) I am, **aren't** I? (informal) I'm not, **am** I?	Yes, you **are**.	No, you **aren't**. No, you **aren't**. No, you **aren't**. No, **you're not**.
You are, **aren't** you? You aren't, **are** you?	Yes, I **am**.	No, **I'm not**. No, **I'm not**.
He is, **isn't** he? He isn't, **is** he? (she)	Yes, he **is**. (she)	No, he **isn't**. No, **he's not**. (she)
There is, **isn't** there? There isn't, **is** there?	Yes, there **is**.	No, there **isn't**. No, **there's not**.
We are, **aren't** we? We aren't, **are** we?	Yes, we **are**.	No, we **aren't**. No, **we're not**.
They are, **aren't** they? They aren't, **are** they?	Yes, they **are**.	No, they **aren't**. No, **they're not**.
There are, **aren't** there? There aren't, **are** there?	Yes, there **are**.	No, there **aren't**.

Modal verbs

Questions	Affirmative answers	Negative answers
Can I can, **can't** I? I can't, **can** I? (you/he/she/it/we/they)	Yes, you **can**. (I/you/he/she/it/we/ they)	No, you **can't**. (I/you/he/she/it/we/ they)
Could I could, **couldn't** I? I couldn't, **could** I? (you/he/she/it/we/they)	Yes, you **could**. (I/you/he/she/it/we/ they)	No, you **couldn't**. (I/you/he/she/it/we/ they)

Questions	Affirmative answers	Negative answers
May (permission) I can, **can't** I? I can't, **can** I? (you/he/she/it/we/they) **May (possibility)** I will, **won't** I? I won't, **will** I? (you/he/she/it/we/they)	Yes, you **may**. (I/you/he/she/it/we/they) Yes, you **may**. (I/you/he/she/it/we/they)	No, you **may not**. (I/you/he/she/it/we/they) No, you **may not**. (I/you/he/she/it/we/they)
Might I will, **won't** I? I won't, **will** I? (you/he/she/it/we/they)	Yes, you **might**.	No, you **might not**.
Must I have to, **don't** I? I don't have to, **do** I? We have to, **don't** we? You have to, **don't** you? He has to, **doesn't** he? (she/it) They have to, **don't** they?	Yes, you **do**. Yes, I **do**. Yes, he **does**. (she/it) Yes, they **do**.	No, you **don't**. No, I **don't**. No, he **doesn't**. (she/it) No, they **don't**.
Should I should, **shouldn't** I? I shouldn't, **should** I? (you/he/she/it/we/they)	Yes, you **should**. (I/you/he/she/it/we/they)	No, you **shouldn't**. (I/you/he/she/it/we/they)
Would I would, **wouldn't** I? I wouldn't, **would** I? (you/he/she/it/we/they)	Yes, you **would**. (I/you/he/she/it/we/they)	No, you **wouldn't**. (I/you/he/she/it/we/they)

Pattern for all other verbs

Questions	Affirmative answers	Negative answers
I do, **don't** I? I don't, **do** I? We do, **don't** we? You do, **don't** you? He does, **doesn't** he? (she/it) They do, **don't** they?	Yes, you **do**. Yes, I **do**. Yes, he **does**. (she/it) Yes, they **do**.	No, you **don't**. No, I **don't**. No, he **doesn't**. (she/it) No, they **don't**.

Present perfect tense
Pattern for all verbs

Questions	Affirmative answers	Negative answers
I have, **haven't** I? I haven't, **have** I? (you/we/they)	Yes, you **have**. (I/we/they)	No, you **haven't**. (I/we/they)
He has, **hasn't** he? He hasn't, **has** he? (she/it)	Yes, he **has**. (she/it)	No, he **hasn't**. (she/it)

Past tense
Be

Questions	Affirmative answers	Negative answers
I was, **wasn't** I? I wasn't, **was** I? We were, **weren't** we?	Yes, you **were**.	No, you **weren't**.
You were, **weren't** you? You weren't, **were** you?	Yes, I **was**. Yes, we **were**.	No, I **wasn't**. No, we **weren't**.
He was, **wasn't** he? He wasn't, **was** he? (she/it)	Yes, he **was**. (she/it)	No, he **wasn't**. (she/it)
There was, **wasn't** there? There were, **weren't** there?	Yes, there **was**. Yes, there **were**.	No, there **wasn't**. No, there **weren't**.

Modal verbs

Questions	Affirmative answers	Negative answers
Can I could, **couldn't** I? I couldn't, **could** I? We could, **couldn't** we? We couldn't, **could** we? You could, **couldn't** you? You couldn't, **could** you?	Yes, you **could**. Yes, I **could**. Yes, we **could**.	No, you **couldn't**. No, I **couldn't**. No, we **couldn't**.
Could I could have, **couldn't** I? I couldn't have, **could** I? We could have, **couldn't** we? We couldn't have, **could** we? You could have, **couldn't** you? You couldn't have, **could** you? He could have, **couldn't** he? He couldn't have, **could** he? (she/it/they)	Yes, you **could have** (**could've**). Yes, you **could have**. Yes, we **could have**. Yes, I **could have**. (she/it/they)	No, you **couldn't have**. No, I **couldn't have**. No, we **couldn't have**. No, he **couldn't have**. (she/it/they)

Questions	Affirmative answers	Negative answers
May **permission** (same as **could**) **possibility** I may have, **right**? I may not have, **right**? We may have, **right**?	Yes, you **may have**.	No, you **may not have**.
You may have, **right**? You may not have, **right**?	Yes, I **may have**. Yes, we **may have**.	No, I **may not have**. No, we **may not have**.
He may have, **right**? He may not have, **right**? (she/it/they)	Yes, he **may have**. (she/it/they)	No, he **may not have**. (she/it/they)
Might I might have, **right**? I might not have, **right**? We might have, **right**? We might not have, **right**?	Yes, you **might have**.	No, you **might not have**.
You might have, **right**?	Yes, I **might have**.	No, I **might not have**.
He might have, **right**? He might not have, **right**? (she/it/they)	Yes, he **might have**. Yes, he **might have**. (she/it/they)	No, he **might not have**. No, he **might not have**. (she/it/they)
Should I should have, **shouldn't** I? I shouldn't have, **should** I? We should have, **shouldn't** we?	Yes, you **should have** (**should've**).	No, you **shouldn't have**.
You should have, **shouldn't** you? You shouldn't have, **should** you?	Yes, I **should have**. Yes, we **should have**.	No, I **shouldn't have**. No, we **shouldn't have**.
He should have, **shouldn't** he? He shouldn't have, **should** he? (she/it/they)	Yes, he **should have**. (she/it/they)	No, he **shouldn't have**. (she/it/they)

Questions	Affirmative answers	Negative answers
Will I would, **wouldn't** I? I wouldn't, **would** I? We would, **wouldn't** we? We wouldn't, **would** we?	Yes, you **would**.	No, you **wouldn't**.
You would, **wouldn't** you? You wouldn't, **would** you? He would, **wouldn't** he? He wouldn't, **would** he? (she/it/they)	Yes, I **would**. Yes, we **would**. Yes, he **would**. (she/it/they)	No, I **wouldn't**. No, we **wouldn't**. No, he **wouldn't**. (she/it/they)
Would I would have, **wouldn't** I? I wouldn't have, **would** I? We would have, **wouldn't** we? We wouldn't have, **would** we?	Yes, you **would have** (**would've**).	No, you **wouldn't have**.
You would have, **wouldn't** you? You wouldn't have, **would** you?	Yes, I **would have**. Yes, we **would have**.	No, I **wouldn't have**. No, we **wouldn't have**.
He would have, **wouldn't** he? (she/it/they)	Yes, he **would have**. (she/it/they)	No, he **wouldn't have**. (she/it/they)

Pattern for all other verbs

Questions	Affirmative answers	Negative answers
I did, **didn't** I? I didn't, **did** I? (you/he/she/it/we/they)	Yes, you **did**. (I/you/he/she/it/we/they)	No, you **didn't**. (I/you/he/she/it/we/they)

Past perfect tense
Pattern for all verbs

Questions	Affirmative answers	Negative answers
I had, **hadn't** I? I hadn't, **had** I? (you/he/she/it/we/they)	Yes, you **had**. (I/you/he/she/it/we/they)	No, you **hadn't**. (I/you/he/she/it/we/they)

Future tense
Pattern for all verbs

Questions	Affirmative answers	Negative answers
I will, **won't** I? I won't, **will** I? (you/he/she/it/we/they)	Yes, you **will**. (I/you/he/she/it/we/they)	No, you **won't**. (I/you/he/she/it/we/they)

Future perfect tense
Pattern for all verbs

Questions	Affirmative answers	Negative answers
I will have, **won't** I? I won't have, **will** I? (you/he/she/it/we/they)	Yes, you **will have**. (I/you/he/she/it/we/they)	No, you **won't have**. (I/you/he/she/it/we/they)

Appendix C
Glossary

have in mind, to, 35, 36, 59
have in store for, to, 1, 7
have one's fingers crossed,
    to, 35, 39
have to, to, 47, 48, 50, 59, 103, 130
have too much on one's plate, 52
heads-up, a, 59, 63
hesitate, to, 69
hesitate, to not, 75
hey, 115, 127
hit the sack, to, 93, 96
honest with you, to be, 13, 17
hopefully, 1, 6, 47
horrible, 13, 94
how about, 13, 48, 51
how about if, 69, 74
how long, 1
how's it going, 127, 131

I

I mean, 25, 27, 59, 103, 105
I try, 35, 37
I'll, 70, 81
I'll bet, 35, 38, 94, 95
I'm, 1
IM, 140
in addition, 82, 104
in front of, 120
in the first place, 25, 27, 81,
    103, 104
in the meantime, 59, 63
in touch, to keep, 40
in town, 1
inside out, 103, 107
instead, 69, 75
is, 3
isn't, 3
it's that, 69, 71, 81

J

jet-lagged, 1
job, to be on the, 38
join, to, 127, 128
junior, 98
just, 1, 3, 25, 35, 71, 81
just sayin', to be, 103, 105
just the opposite, to be, 81
just think, 94, 98

K

keep in mind, 36
keep in touch, to, 40
keep on, 107
kidding, to be, 13, 14
kind of, 1, 13
know, to, 1

L

last minute, at the, 127, 131
last night, 1
late, 13
learn the ropes, to, 127, 132
let me, 71
let someone know, to, 35, 36, 40,
    47, 71
let's, 81, 85
let's say, 48, 51
lift a finger, to not, 81, 84
like, 1, 13, 14, 25, 81
like, to be, 25, 26
like to, would, 13
listen, 48, 52
load off one's mind, to
    be a, 72
load off one's shoulders, to be a,
    69, 72
local scene, 1, 6
look, 48, 51, 59, 69, 103
look forward to, to, 1, 7, 93
look like, to, 47
loose end, to be at a, 132
love, to, 14
love to, to, 13
love to, would, 13

M

make sure, to, 35, 36, 40, 59
make up one's mind, 61
man, 13, 18, 25, 35, 36, 69
matter, the, 81, 83
matter, to, 83
may, 49, 95, 130
may have, 130
maybe, 49, 94, 95
me, too, 35, 36, 40
meeting, 1
mention, not to, 25
might, 49, 94, 95, 130
might have, 130
mill, run of the, 35, 38
mind, 61, 70, 81
mind, change one's, 61
mind, to, 85
mind, to not, 59
miss, to, 69, 72, 127
mix, 1, 5
moment, at the, 1
more of a, 1
must, 50, 130
must be, 1, 13
must have, 130
must not, 50
mustn't, 47

N

neck, to be a pain in the, 115, 118
need, to, 59, 60
never mind, 61
next, 116
no problem, 48, 53
no way, 35, 38, 59, 94, 98
no wonder, 25
none, 59
nonstop schedule, 1, 5
not, 3
not exactly, 81, 86, 89, 103, 107
not mind, to, 59
not to mention, 25
not yet, 129
now and then, 87

O

obviously, 103, 106
of course, 47, 52, 69, 81, 106
oh, 127
oh, dear, 48, 51
oh, yeah, 69, 71
on, 48
on someone's case, to be, 81, 83
on the floor, to be, 35, 38
on the job, to be, 38
on the other hand, 94, 97
on top of it, to be, 69, 72
one more thing, 59, 63
opposite, the, 81, 83, 103
opposite, to be just the, 81
other hand, on the, 94, 97
others, 1
ought to, 50
out of the blue, 81, 84
out there, 59, 62
out to get someone, to be, 81, 83
outside the box, to think, 103, 107
overseas, 94, 98

P

pack light, to, 93, 96
pain in the neck, to be a, 115, 118
paper, 117
party, to, 1
party animal, 1, 4
perfect, 48, 52, 93
pick someone up, 128, 132
pick up, to, 94, 96
pig out, to, 81, 84
plate, have too much on one's, 52
plus, 13, 17, 25, 81, 82, 103, 104
pouring down rain, to be, 115, 118
prefer, to, 13
preferably, 59, 62

prerequisite, 60
pressure, 127, 132
pretty well, 127
pro, 103
probably won't, 95
promise, 1
promise, can, 59
pros, 104
pumped (up), to be, 35, 36, 39, 115, 118
put one's two cents in, to, 103, 107
put someone's name up, to, 107

Q

quite, 25
quite the character, to be, 28

R

rain, to be pouring down, 115, 118
raining cats and dogs, to be, 118
rather, would, 47
ready for, to be, 1
realize, to, 119
really, 1, 13, 25, 27, 35, 59, 81, 106
required to, to be, 60
requirement, 60
ride, to give someone a, 132
right, 1, 2, 47, 52, 60, 92
right away, 47
right now, 13, 59
roomie, 13, 18
run into, to, 35, 36
run of the mill, 35, 38

S

same old thing, the, 94, 97
say, 59, 63
say, to, 16
scene, local, 1, 6
schedule, nonstop, 1, 5
scholarship, 13, 18
second, 115
see you later, 69, 75
seem to, to, 25
senior, 98
senior citizen, 98
shake hands, to, 2
should, 1, 47, 50, 130
should have, 130
shouldn't, 81
show someone a good time, to, 6
show up, 1
show up on someone's doorstep, 7
sick and tired, to be, 81, 84
since, 94, 97, 103, 105, 128
so, 13, 17, 26, 81, 86, 115, 127
so far, 103, 104, 127, 129

Answer key

1   Introducing yourself and others

1·1   1. c   2. b   3. c   4. d   5. a

1·2   1. c, h, n   2. b, k   3. a, e, g, i, l   4. g   5. b, j, k   6. b, l   7. f, l   8. c, h, n
       9. a, m   10. d

1·3   1. Yes, I do./No, I don't.   2. Yes, I am./No, I'm not.   3. Yes, they do./No, they don't.
       4. Yes, I am./No, I'm not.   5. Yes, he (or she) is./No, he (or she) isn't.

1·4   Answers will vary, but questions should begin as follows.   1. Do you . . . ?
       2. Is she . . . ?   3. Are they . . . ?   4. Do you . . . ?   5. Does he . . . ?   6. Are you . . . ?

1·5   1. o   2. q   3. h   4. b   5. i, l   6. a, n   7. k   8. m   9. p   10. c   11. i, l
       12. g   13. r   14. j   15. d, e   16. d, f   17. r

1·6   1. b   2. c   3. a   4. d   5. a

1·7   These are possible answers.   1. What does she do?   2. Thank you.   3. Don't be late!
       4. Tell me about yourself.   5. We finish tomorrow.

1·8   1. see   2. seeing   3. going   4. doing   5. hear

1·9   Answers will vary.

1·10   Answers will vary.

2   Expressing opinions, likes, and dislikes

2·1   1. Would you like to have dinner with me/us?   2. Do you like fast-food restaurants?
       3. Where would you like to go on your vacation?   4. What do you like to do on
       weekends/in the winter/etc.?   5. Do you feel like _____ing?
       6. What kind of fruit do you like?   7. What does he like to do?   8. Does she like
       chocolate ice cream?   9. Do you like _____?   10. Would you
       like to _____?

2·2   1. tell   2. speak   3. tell   4. say   5. tell   6. tell   7. Say   8. say   9. tell
       10. tell   11. tell   12. say

2·3   1. Tell me where you're going.   2. Tell me what they're doing.   3. Tell me how you get
       there.   4. Tell me when you study.   5. Tell me why she's crying.   6. Tell me what
       time we leave.   7. Tell me who you're texting.   8. Tell me how much it costs.

2·4   1. a, b, h, k   2. i, j, p   3. r   4. o   5. c, g   6. n   7. f   8. d, e, l   9. q
       10. c, g, m

2·5   1. c   2. b   3. a   4. d   5. c

2·6   1. a   2. c   3. a   4. b   5. c

2·7   Answers will vary.

2·8   Answers will vary.

2·9   Answers will vary.

3 Describing people, places, and things

3·1 1. b 2. c 3. a 4. c 5. d

3·2 1. What's he like? 2. Does she like _____? 3. What's he like? 4. What do they like to do? 5. What does she like to do? 6. What are you like?

3·3 1. c 2. a,b 3. d 4. i 5. l 6. h 7. j,k 8. e 9. f 10. g

3·4 1. d, i, l, m, n 2. h, j, k 3. c, f 4. b, o 5. a, e, g 6. b, o 7. a, e, g 8. e, g, h

3·5 1. c 2. a 3. d 4. d 5. a

3·6 1. a 2. b 3. d 4. b 5. a

3·7 1. In the first place 2. Second/In the second place 3. Plus 4. Not to mention that

3·8 Answers will vary.

3·9 Answers will vary.

4 Striking up a conversation

4·1 1. There are 2. There are 3. There is 4. There are 5. There is

4·2 1. living 2. live 3. get 4. smoke 5. getting 6. stay 7. working 8. go 9. being 10. driving

4·3 1. a 2. c 3. c 4. b 5. d

4·4 1. b, h, k 2. j 3. e, h 4. i 5. l 6. f 7. d 8. a 9. c 10. e, h

4·5 1. i 2. c 3. d 4. n 5. o 6. a,b 7. g,m 8. f,p 9. j,k 10. e 11. e 12. h 13. l

4·6 1. d 2. b 3. a 4. a 5. b

4·7 1. b, i 2. h 3. j, k 4. a, g, k 5. d 6. f 7. i 8. c, i 9. a, e 10. a, g, l

4·8 Answers will vary.

4·9 Answers will vary.

4·10 Answers will vary.

5 Making dates and appointments

5·1 1. at, in, on, at, in 2. in, at 3. in, at, in 4. on, at, in, at, in 5. on, at, in, at, on, in

5·2 1. May/Can I leave? 2. You mustn't/must not leave. 3. Do you have to work today? 4. You have to work tomorrow. 5. When should I take the medicine? 6. You're supposed to take the medicine just before a meal. 7. You can't/mustn't jaywalk./You're not supposed to cross here. 8. Do I have to/Am I supposed to/Are you supposed to wait for a green light? 9. Would you rather have your steak medium or well done? 10. Will/Can/Could you come to a party at my house on Saturday night? 11. Will/Can you pick me up at the airport? 12. No, I won't pick you up.

5·3 1. p 2. o 3. a 4. a,d 5. d, e, f, g 6. j, k 7. h 8. q 9. m 10. n 11. l 12. b, e, q 13. b 14. d, e, f, g

5·4 1. were 2. could 3. would 4. had 5. didn't 6. were 7. were 8. could 9. called 10. lived

5·5 1. I wish you loved me. 2. I wish my neighbors didn't make so much noise. 3. I wish my mother were here. 4. I wish I were married. 5. I wish she could stay here tonight. 6. I wish he would move his car. 7. I wish she didn't drive so fast. 8. I wish they didn't come home so late. 9. I wish I had enough/more money. 10. I wish our house were bigger./I wish we had a bigger house./I wish we lived in a bigger house.

5·6 1. c 2. a 3. b 4. b 5. c

5·7 1. c, h 2. d, e, i 3. d, e, i, l, m 4. a 5. b, f, j 6. d, e, i, l 7. j 8. k 9. g 10. l

5·8 Answers will vary.

5·9 Answers will vary.

5·10 Answers will vary.

6 Expressing wants and needs

6·1   1. have to   2. need/want   3. want   4. prerequisites   5. would like   6. needs   7. would you mind   8. required to   9. requirements   10. need to/have to

6·2   1. c, h   2. g, k   3. e   4. i, l   5. i, l   6. d   7. f   8. a, b, j   9. m

6·3   1. a   2. c   3. d   4. a   5. d

6·4   Answers will vary.

6·5   1. to mind   2. to have a look   3. to have a mind to   4. none   5. to get rid of   6. to give a heads-up   7. to be worthwhile   8. in the meantime/meanwhile   9. to change your mind   10. utilities   11. One more thing   12. the country   13. go-to person/place   14. say   15. never mind   16. the mind   17. required   18. prerequisite   19. all the bells and whistles   20. out there

6·6   Answers will vary.

7 Making requests and offers

7·1   1. b   2. d   3. a   4. d   5. c   6. d

7·2   1. Would you mind taking off your hat?   2. Would you mind if I borrowed your ladder?   3. Would you mind lending me $20?/Could you (please) lend me $20?   4. Can/Will you lend me $20?   5. Could you please give me directions to the White House?   6. Could/Can I borrow a pen?   7. Come to _____ right away!/Send a fire truck to _____!   8. Could/Can you take me to the airport?   9. Drop me off at the next corner.   10. Turn right at the next stoplight.

7·3   1. Let me help you./Can I help you?   2. I'm taking her home.   3. Is there any way I can help you?/Is there anything I can do to help you?   4. Would you like to borrow some money?/Would you like me to lend you some money?   5. I'll call 911!/I'm calling for an ambulance!   6. Would you like me to water your plants/take care of your dog/etc.?   7. Let me know if I can help you.   8. What can I do for you?/How can I help you?   9. I'll call the police!/I'm calling the police!   10. Can I help you?

7·4   1. c, l   2. e   3. b, k   4. f, g, m   5. o   6. n   7. a, d, h, i, j   8. g

7·5   1. d   2. b   3. a   4. c   5. c

7·6   Answers will vary.

7·7   Answers will vary.

7·8   Answers will vary.

8 Expressing doubts and uncertainty

8·1   1. a. In the first place   b. In addition/Plus   c. plus/in addition   d. As if that weren't enough   e. after all   f. At least/Besides   2. a. In the first place   b. After all   c. Besides   d. As if that weren't enough

8·2   1. besides   2. besides   3. in addition   4. In addition   5. besides

8·3   1. p   2. e   3. d   4. k   5. h   6. f, o   7. c, j, l, n   8. m, r   9. a, b   10. g   11. q   12. i

8·4   1. c   2. b   3. c   4. a   5. b

8·5   1. b   2. c   3. c   4. a   5. b

8·6   1. d   2. b   3. c   4. a   5. b

8·7   Answers will vary.

8·8   1. h   2. k, l   3. j   4. a   5. b, f   6. g   7. c, d, i   8. e

8·9   Answers will vary.

8·10   Answers will vary.

9 Talking about future events

9·1 1. c 2. b 3. d 4. c 5. a 6. c

9·2 1. f 2. j 3. d, h 4. a, c 5. e, g, i 6. b

9·3 1. c 2. a 3. a 4. a 5. c

9·4 1. Still 2. senior 3. the same old thing 4. overseas 5. a whole bunch of 6. freshman
7. pack light 8. catch up on 9. taking care of 10. reach a happy medium/compromise

9·5 Answers will vary.

9·6 Answers will vary.

10 Making a case or arguing a point

10·1 1. a. In the first place b. In the second place/Plus c. Besides/What's more/Furthermore 2. a. In the first place b. In the second place/Plus c. In addition/Plus 3. a. In the first place b. In the second place c. In addition/What's more/Plus d. Furthermore e. Finally/For the frosting on the cake/As if that weren't enough/To top it all off

10·2 1. k 2. b, h 3. i, m, n 4. d, f, g 5. a 6. j, l 7. c 8. e

10·3 1. c 2. b 3. a 4. d 5. a 6. a 7. b 8. d 9. b 10. b

10·4 1. d 2. b 3. a 4. b 5. c 6. c 7. c 8. b

10·5 1. h, o 2. d, i, j, r 3. q 4. c 5. b, l 6. p 7. e 8. a 9. g 10. s 11. n 12. f
13. k 14. m

10·6 Answers will vary.

10·7 Answers will vary.

10·8 Answers will vary.

11 Narrating a story

11·1 1. a. First b. Then c. After that/Next d. Finally 2. a. First b. Then c. Next/After that d. then e. Finally f. For the frosting on the cake/To top it all off/As if that weren't enough

11·2 1. c 2. a 3. c 4. d 5. a

11·3 1. s, x, y 2. h 3. c, i, p, t, u 4. j, w 5. k, l, q, r 6. f, g 7. d 8. v 9. a, b, m, o 10. e, n

11·4 Answers will vary.

11·5 1. a, p 2. g 3. i 4. b, e, j, l 5. h, m, n 6. o, s, t 7. c, q 8. d, f 9. k 10. r

11·6 Answers will vary.

11·7 1. I wish you were here. 2. I wish I could get a promotion at this company. 3. I wish she weren't always stressed out. 4. I wish he knew my e-mail address. 5. I wish they would come to see me.

11·8 1. d 2. a 3. b 4. c 5. c

11·9 Answers will vary.

11·10 Answers will vary.

12 Retelling a conversation

12·1 1. a 2. c 3. b 4. d 5. c 6. b 7. a 8. b

12·2 1. has taken 2. have read 3. haven't finished 4. have already registered 5. have called 6. has never been 7. haven't seen 8. Have you done 9. have already bought 10. Has she gone

12·3 1. he could run it in five minutes 2. we could take thirty minutes 3. It may have rained 4. He might have had the flu 5. You should have paid your bills on time 6. What should I have said when I saw him 7. We had to rearrange the furniture so the piano would fit. 8. The children would pick the wildflowers every spring. 9. It must have been nine o'clock. 10. She left because she had to pick up her daughter.

12·4   1. he was leaving for the beach tomorrow   2. the train always arrived on time   3. they had already eaten lunch   4. the plane had taken off at 9:15   5. they would be here/there in about five minutes

12·5   1. if I had a shovel he could borrow   2. if he would help her with the packages   3. what movie we were going to see   4. why he had called   5. whom she was talking to   6. how far it was   7. if he spoke English   8. when I would come back   9. where she went to school   10. if he wanted her to help him

12·6   1. at the last minute   2. learning the ropes   3. dude, give you a ride   4. pressure   5. at a loose end   6. how's it going   7. babysit   8. end up

12·7   Answers will vary.

12·8   Answers will vary.

13   Electronic conversation

13·1   1. Can you come over as soon as possible?   2. Are you serious? I'm at school. Boring beyond belief.   3. It's over between us. Sorry.   4. Laugh out loud. You're crazy.   5. I'm unhappy without you.   6. Me, too.   7. See you later.   8. Oh my God. She's out to lunch.

13·2   Ansrs wl vry. :)

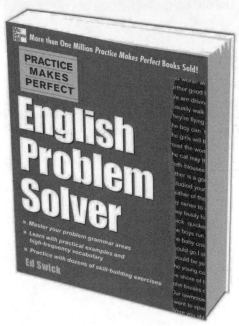
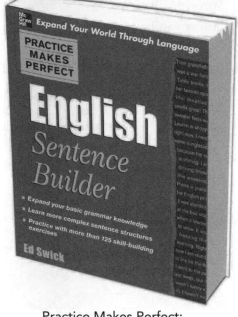
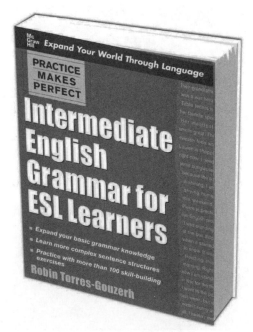
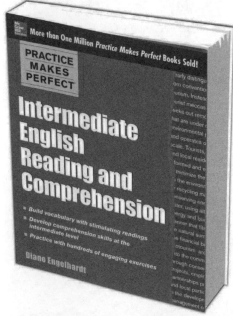